Mmusi Maimane

Mmusi Maimane
....

Prophet or Puppet?

S'THEMBISO MSOMI

Jonathan Ball Publishers
JOHANNESBURG AND CAPE TOWN

All rights reserved.
No part of this publication may be reproduced or transmitted,
in any form or by any means, without prior permission
from the publisher or copyright holder.

© S'thembiso Msomi, 2016

Originally published in South Africa in 2016 by
JONATHAN BALL PUBLISHERS (PTY) LTD
A division of Media24 Limited
P O Box 33977
Jeppestown
2043

ISBN 978-1-86842-708-6
EBOOK 978-1-86842-709-3

Twitter: http://www.twitter.com/JonathanBallPub
Facebook: http://www.facebook.com/pages/Jonathan-Ball-Publishers/298034457992
Blog: http://jonathanball.bookslive.co.za/

Cover design by publicide
Cover image of Mmusi Maimane after his election as DA leader courtesy of
AFP PHOTO / GIANLUIGI GUERCIA
Design and typesetting by Triple M Design, Johannesburg

Printed by *paarlmedia*, a division of Novus Holdings

To my parents,
Sipho and Zine Msomi,
for their teachings and unqualified support

Contents

Introduction: 'With the greatest respect, who are you?' 1
1 A chance encounter 19
2 An ordinary *kasie* boy 40
3 The Obama of Soweto 56
4 The battle of public perceptions 71
5 Dirty tricks in Bethlehem 90
6 'Where we govern, we govern better' 106
7 Jousting against the red berets 122
8 An end to ideology? 134
9 Dress rehearsal for the main event 150

ACKNOWLEDGEMENTS 167
NOTES 171
BIBLIOGRAPHY 185
INDEX 193

INTRODUCTION

....

'With the greatest respect, who are you?'

I AM ONE OF THOSE SCRIBES WITH the dubious honour of having given an opportunity to meet a future president of the United States of America a miss.

It was August 2006 and a little-known US senator, one Barack Obama, was on his way to Cape Town for the start of his Africa Tour ahead of his future announcement that he would be running for the White House.

I had heard and read of him being spoken of as the next US president, but I was sceptical. Not because I doubted the Illinois politician's ability and talent; I had known too little of him to form an opinion on that score. My scepticism mainly stemmed from the 1984 and 1988 US presidential campaigns in which the Reverend Jesse Jackson failed to win nomination as the Democratic Party's candidate.

I remember how my grandfather, Mandlenkosi Absolom Msomi – an avid newspaper reader with a keen interest in American history and politics – would tell his friends that Jackson stood no chance of winning. 'America will never be ready for a Negro as a president,' my grandfather would emphatically state.

Although it was the 1980s and most African-Americans took great offence at being called 'Negroes', my grandfather – born in 1915 – was of that South African generation that grew up believing that being 'Negro' was something to be proud of. His close friend and neighbour, Dixie – nicknamed thus because of his passion for Dixieland music and American Blues – would believe he had paid you a great compliment if he said 'you look like a real Negro, dude' when he spotted you in the street wearing a neat afro, the hairstyle of choice at the time.

So when I read stories of Senator Obama being touted as the future 'first black president' of the United States, I dismissed them as hype.

And then one day my editor at *City Press* called me to his office to ask if I was willing to fly down to Cape Town to attend a function that would be addressed by this American senator with Kenyan roots. The initial invite had been for the editor, but he could not make it due to a prior commitment.

I could not go either. It was an exciting and extremely busy time in South African politics. The ruling African National Congress (ANC) was warring with itself, dragging key state institutions into the fight, as then president Thabo Mbeki and his ANC deputy, Jacob Zuma, raced for the presidency. That month, the Mbeki and Zuma factions were focused on a proxy war that was playing itself out at trade union federation Cosatu, which was preparing for an elective congress. Victory for an election slate headed by Cosatu general secretary Zwelinzima Vavi would be a major boost for Zuma's ambitions, while success at the polls for a faction fronted by the federation's president, Willie Madisha, would have consolidated Mbeki's power.

Our slogan at the newspaper may have been 'Distinctly African', but local politics would still trounce a story about a descendant of Kenyan people who had become an American senator ... even if he was likely to run for the presidency any day. And so I never got to meet the man who was to make history two years later. As I saw visuals of him visiting Nelson Mandela's cell

INTRODUCTION: 'WITH THE GREATEST RESPECT, WHO ARE YOU?'

on Robben Island and addressing various meetings, I felt no regret.

That all changed on 5 November 2008, when the 47-year-old Obama defeated Republican candidate John McCain to become the United States' 44th president and prove my grandfather's statement wrong.

• • •

Before I could learn from it, I had already repeated the mistake.

On a cold and rainy afternoon at the University of Limpopo in Polokwane a few days before Christmas in 2007, a journalist friend had introduced me to a young political activist wearing an ANC Youth League T-shirt and standing alone by one of the entrances to a conference marquee.

The young man was Limpopo's ANC Youth League secretary and one of Youth League president Fikile Mbalula's most trusted lieutenants as he marshalled youth forces behind Zuma's bid for the presidency.

I had known of the youngster from his school days as the reckless president of the ANC's high school student wing, the Congress of South African Students (Cosas). He had shot briefly to national prominence in 2002 by leading a chaotic Cosas march during which pupils went on the rampage, stealing fruit and vegetables from street vendors, robbing people of their cell phones and breaking car windows. In media interviews he gave following the chaotic march, he sounded defiant – like the 1990s Youth League president, the firebrand Peter Mokaba, to whom he was reputed to be close. He was a far cry from the calibre of Cosas leaders my generation had become accustomed to in the early 1990s when a budding intellectual, Thami Rubusana, was president.

The young man's name was Julius Malema. When my colleague introduced us, he referred to him as the next president of the Youth League. I had my doubts. Even though what was unfolding before my eyes at the

Polokwane ANC conference that day had convinced me that Zuma supporters were now in the majority in the party, I still thought the more senior and experienced other candidate for the Youth League job, Saki Mofokeng, would have no difficulty winning the presidency.

In April of the following year, now working for *The Times* newspaper, we were in Bloemfontein to cover the ANC Youth League national conference, billed as a ceremony in which Mbalula's 'young lions' generation – the last generation to have participated directly in the struggle against apartheid – was to hand over the baton to those born in the 1980s.

The handover was chaotic. The conference was delayed for hours due to violent and disruptive conduct from delegates who hurled plastic chairs, bottled water and other dangerous objects at each other. It was a sign of things to come as South Africa entered the post-Polokwane era, which was to fundamentally reshape the political landscape in unexpected ways. Organisers blamed binge drinking and other forms of disorderly conduct for the anarchy. But it was the vote rigging and the manipulation of delegates lists to guarantee a particular outcome in the leadership contest that left many commentators wondering if we were not witnessing the demise of internal democracy within the country's largest political party.

Despite accusations and counter-accusations of malfeasance from competing factions, Malema was declared winner. And thus began a new chapter in South African history that would see him help push Mbeki out of office, scare off the few remaining ANC voters from minority communities with his nationalistic rhetoric, and finally get himself expelled from the party.

But alas, the Obama and Malema instances were not to be the only times I underestimated a political player's chances of reaching the pinnacle.

• • •

INTRODUCTION: 'WITH THE GREATEST RESPECT, WHO ARE YOU?'

It was March 2011 and the country was gearing up for the local government elections. The Democratic Alliance (DA), which was the second biggest political party in the country and the governing party in the Western Cape and the City of Cape Town, had set its sights on winning at least one metro council in Gauteng, South Africa's economic hub.

Zuma's rise to the ANC presidency, coupled with the splitting away of some of the ruling party's ex-leaders to form the Congress of the People (Cope), had weakened the party in urban centres, especially around Gauteng.

The DA hoped that it could translate this disenchantment among the ANC's urban voters into a repeat in Gauteng of what it had done in the Western Cape in 2006, when it won Cape Town. This time the crown jewel was to be Johannesburg. But to win Johannesburg away from the ANC demanded that the DA put forward a credible candidate for mayor – most importantly, one that would appeal to the disillusioned former ANC constituencies.

The DA leader and Western Cape Premier, Helen Zille, was convinced she had found one when she convened a press conference to announce the party's candidates for Johannesburg and Tshwane. I watched the briefing on television with a couple of colleagues and I recall a couple of them shouting '*Who?*' as the DA leader named Mmusi Maimane as the Johannesburg mayoral candidate.

As if she had heard the collective cry, Zille turned at the end of her announcement, still beaming with pride, to face the clean-shaven man with boyish looks seated next to her and said: 'Tell the press corps and the rest of South Africa, to whom you will soon become a household name, who is Mmusi Maimane – and what is his vision for the future?'[1]

No one in the group of journalists I was in took Zille seriously when she claimed that Maimane would be a 'household name'. He was a political novice: no one seemed to have heard of him before. He seemed altogether too lightweight to be credible as a man who would take on the ANC in what had been its stronghold long even before it was unbanned. He appeared too polished – as somebody put it, 'too well-packaged' – to be believable.

Later that afternoon, Maimane was on 24-hour news network eNCA for an interview with Jeremy Maggs, the veteran broadcaster.

'Mr Maimane, good evening to you and with the greatest of respect who are you? You are not a well-known politician; we know that you were born in Soweto, but we know little else,' is how Maggs began the interview.[2]

It seemed that Maimane would disappear from the political arena as quickly as he had appeared. In no time, DA detractors on social media were calling him a 'rent-a-black' candidate and many other unsavoury terms. Even though South Africa was now free and political affiliation according to race was, constitutionally, a thing of the past, association with predominantly white parties such as the DA by a black person was still seen in a particular historical context by some. The country had a long history of 'collaborators' who lent their names to causes that were aimed at derailing the liberation struggle and preserving minority rule. These ranged from Bantustan leaders who accepted 'independence' from the Nationalist government – hence perpetuating the system of apartheid – to politicians like John Gogotya who, as the apartheid government faced increasing international isolation and pressure, sought to discredit the struggle for freedom by agreeing to be paraded as the black 'supporters' of the National Party.

Maimane was acutely aware of this accusation from the onset. During his mayoral campaign launch rally speech in Kliptown, Soweto, he sought to convince locals that joining a historically white political party should not be considered taboo in a democratic South Africa: 'I know that for many of you, making this change will take much courage. On my path to this stage in Soweto, I too have had to face my fears, and confront the criticism of others … We need the courage to stand for the future, and not allow our past to hold us hostage,' he said.

INTRODUCTION: 'WITH THE GREATEST RESPECT, WHO ARE YOU?'

The elections came and went, with Maimane failing to unseat the ANC in Johannesburg. But he did not vanish from the political scene as expected; instead he grew in stature. He was elected the DA's caucus leader in Johannesburg, a post party leaders would use to test his mettle. Over a year later, Zille made him the DA's national spokesperson – a position that had been held by popular MP Lindiwe Mazibuko before she became the party leader in Parliament. It was a significant promotion; past DA spokespeople had gone on to hold prominent positions in the party – Zille and Mazibuko being the most obvious examples.

Did that mean that Maimane, too, was headed for the greater heights? Zille certainly thought so: 'He has the leadership qualities, the vibrancy, the perseverance and the will to lead. In the coming months you … will get to know him well.'[3]

Even with this high praise from Zille, we never suspected that Maimane's rise to the very top of the party hierarchy would happen so quickly.

Zille had never hidden her belief that, in order for the DA to grow and become a viable alternative to the ANC, it needed to become more representative of the country's demographics at leadership level. However, while it had become clear even at that early stage that Maimane was one of the most gifted orators post-apartheid South Africa has seen so far, his lack of extensive experience in politics put him below many party leaders and activists in terms of the pecking order. If Zille did step down sometime after the 2014 election, as was being speculated within some DA quarters, the likes of Lindiwe Mazibuko, Athol Trollip, Patricia de Lille and Wilmot James looked to me to be better placed to have a bite at federal leadership.

When, soon after the 2014 general election in which Maimane unsuccessfully ran for the Gauteng premiership, a political analyst suggested that the reputed R100 million the DA spent on the campaign had turned Maimane into the most recognised DA face after Zille, I did not take him seriously.

Barely a year later, on Sunday, 10 May, I watched on television as Zille broke the news to the delegates to the party's federal congress at the Boardwalk Conference Centre in Port Elizabeth, Eastern Cape.

'Your new leader,' she said, slowly opening the white envelope containing the name of the winner, 'is Mmusi Maimane!'

There was a spontaneous roar from delirious delegates. As Maimane appeared on stage in a blaze of fireworks, some delegates could not hide their excitement as they rushed to hug and kiss him. History had been made. The Democratic Alliance – a party whose roots are steeped in the opposition tradition of the whites-only Parliament of bygone years – had elected its first black leader.

To some of Maimane's supporters the significance of the victory was further amplified by the fact that 10 May was the twenty-first anniversary of Nelson Mandela's inauguration as South Africa's first black president. At the age of 34, Maimane had beaten his challenger, respected academic and outgoing DA federal chairperson Wilmot James, by winning 88.9 per cent of the votes.

The landslide victory marked the start of a new era for the DA. It was the party's Obama moment.

'South Africa needs transformation and Mmusi Maimane is the person to lead that transformation,' university student and DA supporter Lutho Sokudela had told the *Daily Maverick*'s Greg Nicolson just before voting started.[4] Sokudela's sentiments were shared by many others who believed that Maimane's election had put an end to accusations – mainly by ANC supporters – that the DA was a 'white' party concerned only with 'preserving white privilege'.

Fully aware of these accusations and how the perception of the DA as a 'white' party had harmed its growth potential in past elections, Maimane wasted no time in re-defining the party's vision under his leadership. While he put non-racialism at the centre of this vision, he stressed to delegates that 'non-racialism does not mean being colour-blind'. 'We cannot pretend that

INTRODUCTION: 'WITH THE GREATEST RESPECT, WHO ARE YOU?'

apartheid never happened,' he said. 'We cannot ignore the fact that apartheid was a system that defined us by the colour of our skin. It was a system that could put a pencil through your hair. A system that dictated where you could live, where you could work and who you could marry.'[5]

By acknowledging the evils of apartheid, Maimane was sending a message that his party was not going to be a home for apartheid apologists: the accusation that DA leaders hankered for the past system of racial segregation was simply not true.

Whereas many of the past DA leaders and those of its predecessor, the Democratic Party, often argued that a non-racial South Africa should be one that is 'colour-blind', Maimane rejected this: 'I simply don't agree with those who say they don't see colour,' he said. 'Because, if you don't see that I'm black, then you don't see me.'

However, the acknowledgement of the racial differences and the damage caused by the apartheid experience did not mean that skin colour must define South Africans forever, he said. 'The system of racial classification devised by Hendrik Verwoerd was evil and deplorable, and we cannot stay trapped in that way of thinking. We must triumph over the evil of apartheid by building a new bridge into a new future. We must not remain victims of our yesterday, we must believe in tomorrow.'

For DA sympathisers and non-partisans alike, it was a moving and seminal speech, a breath of fresh air in the context of a South Africa that seemed to be increasingly polarised by race and drifting away from the 1994 dream of racial unity. In no time conversations about the new DA leader had shifted from dismissing him as the party's flavour of the month to serious questions as to whether, like Obama, he could go all the way and become president of his nation. Commentators were waxing lyrical about his bucket-loads of charisma; his ability to fluently speak six South African languages; the fact that he was smart and savvy, well-educated and good-looking to boot.

That his wife was white and their children mixed-race meant that he would be 'non-threatening' to the DA's core constituencies while having no difficulty reaching out to new ones, some commentators remarked. The days of *'with the greatest respect, who are you?'* now seemed like an ancient past.

• • •

That Maimane was now a household name was put beyond doubt three days after his election when he held a Twitter town hall under the hash tag: #AskMmusi. The town hall was supposed to be an opportunity for Maimane's followers to get to know him better by asking him about his background, his beliefs and values, and his plans as the official opposition's new leader. The communication team that came up with the concept could not have imagined that #AskMmusi would end up being number two on the worldwide Twitter trends of that day.

True to the spirit of the South African Twitterati, the questions quickly morphed from the serious and engaging, to the highly critical, and then the absurd and outright funny. Among the more serious tweets were questions posed to Maimane about how he planned to take the Nkandla fight forward and whether his election meant that the DA would now be 'a black party'.

'@MmusiMaimane honestly how are you going to get more people to vote for you? And especially how are you gonna get the white folk? #AskMmusi,' tweeted @guillClark.

To which Maimane responded: 'We don't mobilise on the basis of race. Our values of Freedom, Fairness, Opportunity are central to the DA.'

@thabilelr wanted to know the DA leader's stance on social grants and the issuing of birth certificates to South African-born children with foreign parents.

INTRODUCTION: 'WITH THE GREATEST RESPECT, WHO ARE YOU?'

'I support social grants as a safety net for the poor. The hard work is to grow the economy for more jobs #AskMmusi,' Maimane responded.

Others quizzed him about Black Economic Empowerment, with @ntsikamsuthu even charging that the DA was openly opposed to the policy.

Maimane replied: 'The DA has always supported measures of redress. We want a BEE that creates jobs not a few connected people.'

@ladyj_oy wanted Maimane to 'break down in your words what Allister Sparks meant about Verwoerd being smart ...' (Sparks, a veteran journalist, had caused a massive uproar on the first day of the federal congress when he counted apartheid architect Hendrik Verwoerd as among the 'smart' politicians he had encountered during his 64-year career as a newspaperman. His comment, made during an address to delegates at the congress, immediately became ammunition for DA opponents who said it was evidence that party leaders and supporters still longed for apartheid.)

Maimane responded to @ladyj_oy by tweeting: 'I disagreed with him and he has already apologised. Verwoerd's policies are deplorable and evil. #AskMmusi'.

And then there were those who were suspicious of the new DA leader, like @cenanda808 who wanted to know Maimane's response to accusations that he was a 'puppet or token for the DA'.

'I've worked hard to get where I am. The puppet and token insults are manufactured by a very desperate ANC,' Maimane retorted.

But then things got absurd and joke tweets flooded Maimane's timeline.

When multi-award-winning American pop star Beyoncé sang 'I know she was attractive but I was here first', who was she talking about, @Tshepol_ demanded to know.

To which Maimane coolly responded: 'You'll need to ask her' and then cc'd @Beyonce in his reply.

He didn't bother to answer others like @VIVLifestyle who wanted to know the home address of 'the guy who presses the load shedding button' or @freemantle who asked: 'Why did Bob Marley shoot the Sheriff but not the Deputy'.

Then there was @lulu_luwela, who touched on the probably thorny, and yet light, issue which continues to divide black and white on university campuses, schools and work-places: the air-conditioner.

'Under your leadership, will black people finally get the air con remote??! #AskMmusi'. The DA leader is yet to answer this pertinent question.

Others like @iAmKudz playfully employed popular stereotypes about black households to suggest that Maimane may not possess what today's Hip-Hop generation would call township 'street-cred': 'Is it true that all the Country Fresh ice cream tubs in your household ACTUALLY contain ice cream and not leftovers?'

Even well-known ANC personalities and supporters could not miss out on all the fun.

'If you are Obama of Soweto, can I be the Mmusi of Mdantsane,' asked Khaya Dlanga, while Home Affairs department spokesman Mayihlome Tshwete wanted to know why mothers used to 'make us fetch the stick they gave us hidings with' and whether Maimane did not think this was mean of them.

The Twitter response, the biggest for a South African politician on social media, was by no means an indication of how Maimane and the DA were to perform in future elections. It did, however, indicate that as a leader he would not be easy to ignore.

• • •

Although a talented public speaker who already had a number of memorable

INTRODUCTION: 'WITH THE GREATEST RESPECT, WHO ARE YOU?'

speeches under his belt when he ran for the DA leadership, there were always questions about Maimane's ability to hold his own in a political space dominated by such large personalities as Zuma and the rabble-rousing Malema, who now had his own party – the Economic Freedom Fighters (EFF).

From the very first day they set foot in Parliament as MPs, comparisons began to be made. With just less than a year separating them – Maimane was born on 6 June 1980 and Malema on 3 March 1981 – some analysts had begun speculating that a future South African president would emerge between them. Maimane had the massive machinery of a political party that had grown with every election and was showing no signs of reaching its ceiling yet. In contrast, Malema was leading a newly founded political party with no track record to speak of and whose staying power was yet to be tested. It had gained its place in Parliament, garnering the third-largest number of votes after the ANC and the DA, largely on the back of urban youth's disgruntlement with the Zuma administration and its failure to deliver on its jobs promise.

Prior to the EFF's formation, the Congress of the People – another breakaway from the ANC – had benefited greatly from the same disillusionment only to see its electoral base diminish soon after. But what the EFF lacked in organisational strength and pedigree it made up for with the sheer strength of Malema's larger-than-life personality and the party's obstreperous behaviour.

That the leadership styles of the two young leaders would sharply differ was evident on the day the fifth democratic Parliament debated Zuma's first State of the Nation Address of his second term as President. In a column titled 'Maimane charms Zuma while Malema turns up the heat',[6] *City Press* political editor Rapule Tabane described the contrasting styles of the two leaders in great detail.

According to the article, before the official start of the parliamentary session on that day, Maimane had walked across to the President's bench to shake his hand and engage in small talk. Malema, a one-time fiery Zuma supporter who even once promised to 'kill for Zuma', made no such gesture to the man he had not spoken to since his expulsion from the ANC three years earlier.

When the time for the debate arrived, Maimane began his speech by wishing Zuma – who had taken leave a few weeks earlier due to a health scare – good health: 'This was in contrast to Malema whose speech was full of vitriol ... and full of loathing for Zuma,' commented Tabane.[7]

In weeks and months that followed, more comparisons were made. As EFF antics led to one session of Parliament or the other being abandoned, Malema appeared to be getting all the public attention while Maimane was reduced to insignificance.

'Julius Malema: the real leader of the opposition,'[8] wrote Gareth van Onselen in a column that expressed what seemed to be a popular sentiment at the time. Regular callers to radio talk shows began talking about how Malema and his red berets had made parliamentary debates 'exciting' with their combative style that almost always ended with the House degenerating into chaos.

As Leader of the Opposition, Maimane was expected to be setting the opposition agenda in the National Assembly, but his gentlemanly approach to crisis – which often meant trying to find a middle ground while the EFF and the ANC tore into each other – made him lose the initiative. Ahead of Zuma's appearances before the House to answer questions, media houses would be running with stories anticipating Malema's next move, and not Maimane's.

Malema had become a de facto leader of the opposition. In his column, Van Onselen pointed to an incident during an August parliamentary session in which Zuma dismissively refused to respond to 'a non-issue' raised by Maimane because 'your question really is not a question'. 'You can see

INTRODUCTION: 'WITH THE GREATEST RESPECT, WHO ARE YOU?'

Maimane politely nodding as Zuma fobs him off,' he wrote, '... you can see Zuma pointing aggressively at Maimane, putting him in his place ... From the moment his question ended, he was a passive, even submissive observer.'[9]

When Malema's turn came to quiz Zuma about when he planned to 'pay back the money' used to upgrade his family home in Nkandla to the tune of R246 million, the President gave him an answer the EFF leader would not accept. And so he became more aggressive, telling Zuma: 'We want the date of when you are paying the money.' ANC MPs objected on the President's behalf, telling the Speaker, Baleka Mbete, that Zuma had already answered the question, but Malema was undaunted: 'These things of points of order are the ones that you are hiding behind,' he said, pointing at Zuma.

For Van Onselen, the whole saga – which ended with proceedings being suspended due to EFF MPs refusing to have Zuma speak until he answered their question – was indicative of Zuma seeing Maimane 'as an annoyance': 'He does not take him or his questions seriously and fears no reprisal; nor does he have reason to,' he wrote.[10]

But DA MP Makashule Gana said it was unfair to single out Maimane as having been overshadowed by Malema, as even the ANC, with its huge majority in the National Assembly, often did not know how to react to the EFF leader: 'We did not foresee Parliament going to that direction of becoming rowdy ... It is always a challenge as we are no longer the only dominant player there on the opposition benches. We have a situation in the opposition ranks where there is a competitor who is fiercely competitive and their tactics are very different from ours.'[11]

Since then, however, Maimane's stature has grown in Parliament. Whereas for a while he seemed to be struggling to step out of Malema's shadow, sometimes even yielding to the temptation of adopting the EFF's belligerent approach to parliamentary engagement, by his second year as Leader of the

Opposition in Parliament he appeared to be regaining the initiative.

DA insiders say their internal polls show that the party's core supporters are turned off by Malema-like antics and want their MPs to continue with their robust engagement with the executive without being 'rude' and disruptive. Mimicking the EFF's tactics would be to the detriment of the DA, argued Gana, as it would result in a dysfunctional parliament where the party would not be able to fulfil its role of holding the cabinet to account: 'The temptation to try and be like EFF is sometimes there. But we say if we go that way it won't really work for us. By remaining calm and cool even under provocation, we get things done. We can't afford a failing parliament.'

The DA has been able to distinguish itself from the EFF by insisting on being more than about Nkandla. It has sought to initiate debate on a variety of issues ranging from the quality of water, to government's appetite for a seemingly unaffordable nuclear build programme, to the collapse of governance in a number of parastatals and other government-owned institutions. Outside of Parliament, the DA under Maimane has used the courts effectively to force government and the ANC to change decisions they took using their majority in Parliament even though such decisions were contrary to the law and inconsistent with the Constitution. The question, however, is whether these court victories, coupled with the party's role in Parliament, will help the DA grow beyond the 30 per cent mark in the next general election, and to a majority party by 2024.

Maimane is cautious about publicly putting a percentage to his election targets. On 16 July 2015, he addressed a well-attended British Chamber of Business in Southern Africa evening meeting at the exclusive Inanda Club in Sandton. When the question was put to him as to when he expected the DA to be in power, he said he anticipated the party to be part of the central government in 2024.

INTRODUCTION: 'WITH THE GREATEST RESPECT, WHO ARE YOU?'

He suggested that this would be a coalition government, with the DA as the largest party, and set out a couple of values which, he said, would guide that government. 'The first one is don't mobilise on the basis of race,' he said. 'So there will be no coalition with parties who mobilise on that score. Secondly we need to professionalise the state. There will be no coalition with any party that believes in cadre deployment. Thirdly, this coalition will be based on belief in the market economy as well as defending the rule of law.'[12]

His optimism about the DA ascending to power by 2024, he said, stemmed from the belief that South Africa was now faced with the same kind of economic crisis that 'had brought about accelerated political change' in the early 1990s. But does he expect this change to catapult him into the presidency by then? He gave a diplomatic answer: 'My work is to build consensus.'[13]

• • •

When I was commissioned to write this book, I had already begun to study Maimane closely in an attempt to understand how he rose so rapidly to lead the party despite being initially written off by much of the commentariat as a hired hand who had been put in place in a desperate attempt to convince Johannesburg voters that the DA was a party for all.

His May 10 victory in Port Elizabeth had convinced me that this church pastor was to play an important role in our politics for years to come, especially when considering that age was very much on his side.

But what was his politics? Was he the post-liberation-struggle prophet bestowed with the mission to lead South Africa out of the morass of underdevelopment and corruption the country finds itself in, two decades after the fall of apartheid?

Or was he a puppet, elected to the post of federal leader by a party that realised that without a black leader it would never be able to grow beyond its largely white and limited base?

CHAPTER 1

A chance encounter

It was at a McDonald's outlet on Rivonia Road in Sandton that Mmusi Maimane finally put his signature down on a Democratic Alliance membership form and paid his R10 joining fee. There was no fanfare to mark the occasion: he was running a business consultancy at the time and was rushing for his appointment with his next client.[1] But for Ian Ollis, who had spent three years trying to reel him in, that afternoon in 2010 must have been deeply satisfying, little though he – or Maimane – could have foreseen the consequences.

When Maimane shook Ollis's hand at the end of their short encounter, he could not have imagined that within five years, following in the footsteps of Helen Zille and Tony Leon, he would take up the reins of a party with a long and illustrious history on the opposition benches; a party whose past leaders include such luminaries of the South African liberal tradition as Helen Suzman, Frederik van Zyl Slabbert and Zach de Beer.

Certainly, the then 30-year-old could not have thought that by his thirty-fifth birthday, sections of society would be seriously considering him as a potential future president and that on his broad shoulders would fall the

Herculean task of winning millions of traditional ANC voters over to the DA.

In 2007, the same year in which Maimane first met Ollis, DA MP Joe Seremane had failed in his bid to succeed Leon as party leader.[2] Despite having been the most recognisable black face during Leon's tenure as federal leader, he could only muster 65 votes to Zille's 786 at the DA's May 2007 congress. Even Athol Trollip, provincial leader in the Eastern Cape, received more votes (228) than Seremane.

If Seremane, who had served six years on Robben Island and had an impeccable record as a political activist, could not win the election, then the DA was still light years from having a black leader, conventional wisdom went. But a closer observation of the changes in the DA, especially since Zille took over, reveals a systematic shift in the party's growth strategy to focus on an aggressive recruitment and training drive mainly targeted at young and black potential activists.

Much of this shift in focus was personally driven by Zille's desire to turn the historically white DA into a party with mass and black appeal.[3] She seems to have understood from the outset that if the DA was to grow to become a real threat to the ANC at the polls nationally, its upper leadership echelons would have to become more representative.

• • •

Maimane, however, did not come to the party through the DA's formal recruitment network and its well-structured leadership training programme. It was by chance, almost.

It all began with a tragedy. An unidentified homeless woman drowned during a rainstorm while sleeping in one of the parks in Johannesburg's northern suburbs. The shocking incident jolted Ollis into action. He was a DA ward councillor at the time for an area that included Rosebank, Craighall and parts of Sandton. He approached the City of Johannesburg and said: 'What are you doing about people who are sleeping in the parks and bus shelters? What is the policy in terms of housing and what are you going to do for these people?'[4] The City wrote back to him, essentially washing its hands of the matter.

South Africa prides itself on being one of a few countries around the world to provide free housing for the poor. But there is still no clear policy catering for those regarded as part of the social underclass.[5] To be considered for a free government house, commonly known as an 'RDP house', one would have to earn anything from nothing to R3 500 a month, the City of Johannesburg told Ollis. But, City officials added, there was no policy to prioritise paupers who slept in the streets on its notoriously long waiting list for housing.

Frustrated, Ollis began looking elsewhere for solutions. If the City and the government were not going to do anything, he would try the churches and non-governmental organisations in his ward. He held a series of meetings with religious leaders and representatives of NGOs operating in the wards and its surroundings. It was at one of these meetings, in late 2007, that a tall young man with a chocolate skin tone walked through the doors of the Rosebank Union Church on William Nicol Drive, Sandton. He sat next to Ollis and introduced himself as Aloysias Maimane from the Liberty Church in Randburg. In business and on church-related matters, Maimane almost always introduced himself as Aloysias, hardly ever as Mmusi.[6]

Aloysias and Ollis almost immediately hit it off. 'After the meeting we agreed to go and have coffee, chat and get to know each other. That started a conversation with him,' remembered Ollis.

They met for coffee, and sometimes breakfast, quite regularly in 2008 and

2009 as their relationship blossomed into a friendship. Although the conversations were initially about finding ways to provide shelter for the homeless, politics would soon dominate.

This was a period of major political upheavals and uncertainty in South Africa. Just days before Christmas in 2007 at Mankweng township in Polokwane, Limpopo, President Thabo Mbeki – a politician Maimane readily admits to have greatly admired – suffered a humiliating defeat at the hands of his rival, Jacob Zuma, in the battle for ANC presidency.[7]

Zuma's victory was to precipitate a chain of political developments that would change South Africa for good.[8]

Nine months after the Polokwane Conference, and following a contentious Pietermaritzburg High Court ruling that was later to be overturned by higher courts, Zuma engineered Mbeki's unceremonious recall from the Union Buildings.[9] Although Mbeki's removal from office – ostensibly because Judge Chris Nicholson had found that he politically meddled with Zuma's corruption case – was relatively peaceful, it caused much indignation among his supporters within and outside the ANC. Mbeki was a few months from finishing his second, and final, term as Head of State when the ANC National Executive Committee demanded that he stepped down.[10]

Among those who found the ANC decision unjust was Maimane. He was not active in politics at the time but considered himself to be an ANC supporter. Newspaper editor and columnist Fikile-Ntsikelelo Moya, who has known Maimane since he was a little boy, believes that the DA leader was one of many young South Africans who were 'galvanised into politics' by what the then imminent Zuma presidency symbolised for them.[11]

Zuma had risen to power despite a dark cloud of over 700 corruption and fraud charges – some related to the Arms Deal – hanging over him. A mere three years before being voted the country's fourth president, he had been before the south Gauteng High Court defending himself on a rape charge.

He was acquitted, but not before making damaging statements, from the witness box, about taking a shower as a form of protection against possible HIV infection and suggesting that he was culturally obliged to have sex with a woman once she had shown interest in having him.

For a devout Christian like Maimane, who had married young and regarded the institution of marriage as sacrosanct, Zuma's utterances would have been repulsive. By contrast, Mbeki was always a hero in Maimane's eyes. Even before he expressed his interest in taking up politics as a career, he would passionately defend Mbeki's leadership style and choices in his many debates with his childhood friend, Thabo Shole-Mashao, who remembered that 'after having read Mark Gevisser's book, we would spend a lot of time debating Mbeki. He used to be attracted to his leadership style, he was his hero'.[12]

Years later, now having risen to become the DA's national spokesman and leader of its City of Johannesburg caucus, Maimane publicly displayed his affection for the former president by leaving his seat in the National Assembly's public gallery and heading for the VIP section where Mbeki was seated to take a selfie. Mbeki's broad smile in the picture, which Maimane posted on social media almost immediately, suggested he had no qualms about being photographed with the spokesman of a party that had been a thorn in his side for most of his presidency.

The occasion was the February 2014 official opening of Parliament, a day that traditionally belongs to the incumbent president who sets the political tone for the incoming year by delivering his State of the Nation Address. That Maimane chose the occasion to publicly associate himself with the very person Zuma had pushed out of power was seen as a well-calculated move. Radio journalist Stephen Grootes, who witnessed the incident from the press gallery at the opposite end of the House, analysed the move thus: 'In retrospect, this could have been evidence that actually this was part of a very well and long ago thought-through strategy. That if in 2014 you wanted to target those who voted for Cope in 2009, you had to start early. And then, as Zuma has continued to distance himself in one way from the ANC of Mbeki (in terms of corruption), you would start to stake your claim more and more often, in more and more obvious ways.'[13]

But Shole-Mashao, who spent some time with his friend Maimane in the hours leading up to the State of the Nation Address that evening, takes a less cynical view of his motives. On ascertaining that Mbeki would make what was by then a rare appearance in the National Assembly for Zuma's speech, Maimane had told his friend that there was nothing more he wanted that evening than to take a picture with Mbeki, the politician he had always admired.[14]

• • •

Maimane was too young to have participated in the struggle against apartheid, though in an interview with *Destiny Man*, a South African glossy magazine targeted at young and upwardly mobile black males, he spoke about participating in protest marches at 13, even admitting to making a petrol bomb.[15] Elsewhere, he told the fashion bible *GQ South Africa* that 'I was a comrade' during the period of conflict between the ANC-dominated Dobsonville township and the then IFP-controlled single-sex hostel nearby. The hostel in question was a few blocks away from Maimane's home. Where it used to be now stands a block of residential flats, the hostel having been demolished during the violence that engulfed many townships and informal settlements in Johannesburg and surrounding areas as politicians negotiated a new political dispensation for the country in the early 1990s.

Even though he was barely a teenager, Maimane would have witnessed some of the attacks between hostel dwellers – who were almost exclusively Zulu-speaking migrant workers – and the rest of township residents. His memories were vivid: 'My own experiences of conflict and violence were closer to home, in the township, where a war was happening between the IFP, ANC and other groups ... I grew up *ke le Motswana* (speaking seTswana), the tongue of my father. Because of the proximity to so much violence, I do concede that I did in fact fear Zulus as a child. And yet today I speak isiZulu fluently even though the languages of my household were seTswana and isiXhosa.'[16]

In September 1992, *City Press* reported on how the internecine conflict had forced residents of Jonas Moabi and Luthuli Streets, which are not far from Maimane's home on Mmutle Street, to flee their homes: 'Residents claim that fear has gripped every facet of their lives and they do not dare walk in these streets at night or even during the day. They claim that although the hostel may seem deserted, sporadic shootings directed at township residents come from the direction of the hostel.'[17] The young Maimane would have seen some of his neighbours, after they drove IFP supporters out of the township, vandalising the hostel and looting what remained of its walls, windows and doors to be used later as material to help them extend their homes.[18]

Although Kgotla Molefe, who is two years older than Maimane and grew up just across the street from the Maimanes, does not remember an instance when they would have had to make petrol bombs, he does recall attending local ANC meetings with him: 'We were kids, he must have been 13 or 14. There used to be big ANC meetings and we would go.'[19]

But such meetings were not a big part of the life of the child Fikile-Ntsikelelo Moya remembers: 'He was not really political, he was too young for that. When he was of matured enough age to get involved, it was already post 1990 ... Even then he was never the one who would have been picked to be a political activist. His youth was defined mainly by his religious inclinations.'[20] However Moya does acknowledge that even at that young age, Maimane's world view would have been partly influenced by the political environment that prevailed in Soweto and its surroundings. Throughout their formative years, the sprawling township was a hive of political activity with many of the people who helped raise them up playing activist roles of one type or another.

One such person was Sister Christine Obotseng, who taught Maimane at St Angela's Primary School in Dobsonville.[21] The nun had been one of the most prominent anti-apartheid activists in Soweto during the 1980s and, for her activities, was detained several times with the likes of Nomvula Mokonyane – who is now water and sanitation minister – and the late ANC MP Sister Bernard Ncube.[22]

For Moya and many of his peers who were under her tutelage some eight years before Maimane, Sister Christine was an inspiration and awakened their political consciousness. She did the same for Maimane: 'She had a deep faith but a strong sense of black consciousness. She would say you are black and strong and good enough to compete with anyone. She was an ANC activist, a phenomenal individual who died a few years ago,' he told *Noseweek*, 'She'd hold open discussions in her office in the afternoons on a whole range of issues, and I'd go straight to her office after school just to talk.'[23]

Sister Christine, remembers Shole-Mashao, was a strict disciplinarian who was feared by all the children at St Angela's: 'But she was also very political. Mmusi and I used to spend a whole lot of time with her after school. She would buy us cookies and cold drinks. She was socialising us politically through letting us study and analyse [poet] Mzwakhe Mbuli's "The Spear Has Fallen".'[24]

Sister Christine would also make her pupils at the school read the now defunct Catholic Church-owned *New Nation* newspaper, an alternative publication edited by one of struggle stalwart Walter Sisulu's sons, Zwelakhe. The

New Nation, perhaps more than any other newspaper in Johannesburg, was regarded as the mouthpiece of the liberation movement in the late 1980s and early 1990s. For its uncompromising investigative journalism that sought to expose the brutality of the apartheid police state and promote the aims and objectives of the then banned ANC and other struggle formations, the newspaper was restricted and banned several times by the state.[25]

'She used to make us read the *New Nation* even if we didn't know all the words. She would later explain to us what those words meant,' remembered Shole-Mashao.

On a few occasions, Shole-Mashao said, they did see Sister Christine being detained for her political activities. Witnessing such arrests would have further made Maimane and his schoolmates aware of the political situation in the country, even though their young age would have meant they would not fully comprehend the reasons. She would spare very little detail when telling them about the torture and psychological abuse she and her fellow anti-apartheid activists endured while in police detention. In one instance, Sister Christine shared with the young Maimane and Shole-Mashao the worst humiliation she and her fellow women detainees were subjected to every month.[26] When authorities realised that a detainee was menstruating, they would deliberately deny her access to water for ablution purposes, hence putting her health at risk. The story not only shocked Maimane and Shole-Mashao, but also made at least one of them acutely aware of one of the seldom spoken about health problems confronting young women from poor backgrounds.

It was not until he visited the United States in 2010 and had a chance discussion with an African-American woman from a disadvantaged background that Shole-Mashao decided to do something about the lack of access to sanitary towels for young women from impoverished households: 'What Sister Christine told me that day more than two decades ago revisited me when this

African-American woman told me about sanitary towels in her neighbourhood and how this takes away the dignity of many women,' he said.[27]

As a result, in 2011, Shole-Mashao – by then an established radio producer – started the Thusa a Girl Child (TaGC) movement, which distributes such towels to those in need in the hope that, among other things, this would help reduce the number of girls forced to drop out of school because of their lack of access to such basic necessities.

As Shole-Mashao's initiative demonstrates, Sister Christine's pro-liberation movement teachings and stories must have left a lasting impression on the minds of the two young men.

• • •

With this kind of background, it is no wonder that, despite his burgeoning friendship with Ollis, Maimane still found it hard to readily join the DA. Ollis remembers: 'I said to him that he must join the DA and he said he was considering it but had a lot of questions. It took us three years of breakfast and coffee and lots of questions for him to be sure that this was the right decision to make.'[28]

Among the issues Maimane was most concerned about was the party's policy towards Black Economic Empowerment (BEE) and affirmative action. He grilled Ollis on whether the DA mainly represented the interests of big business, as his passion was to see small and medium-sized enterprises grow. According to Ollis, 'We met about 15 times, maybe, to discuss these issues. He is not easily co-opted onto someone else's agenda. He did not believe everything I told him, for example, he went to ask other people. He is quite independent.'

Among those he consulted was Patricia de Lille who, at the time, had begun the process of folding her own political party, the Independent Democrats, into the DA. De Lille had formally joined the DA in August 2010 and Maimane asked to meet her in Johannesburg later that year to understand why she had chosen to disband the party she had established on her own and join what was once a rival political party.

'When I met him for the first time he was still grappling with the idea of whether he should join the DA,' remembers De Lille. 'One of the conversations we had was how I found myself in the DA. I told him that I had had a special goal in life of being the first woman to start her own party and I succeeded. I also told him that politics was not static and that flashlights were starting to flicker [signalling danger in the political system, she meant] and that I wanted to be part of an alternative to the ANC.'[29]

This was during the period of Zille's grand idea of the 'realignment of politics' whereby, she predicted, the 'outcome will be a two-party system in South Africa, where power can change hands peacefully through the ballot box'.[30] The 'nucleus of one of the two major parties' would be the DA, and the other, the ANC. Besides the ID, other parties involved in the 'realignment' talks with the DA were Bantu Holomisa's United Democratic Movement and the Mosiuoa Lekota faction of the then divided Cope.

According to De Lille, what impressed her and other DA personalities Maimane interacted with during this period was that, even though he had not made up his mind to join, 'he had made a conscious decision that he wanted to do more for his country'. In addition, she said, 'He also had his own ideas of what he wanted to do. For instance he impressed on me the need for non-racialism. He had read up on what happened in 1956 and was very impressed with what had happened during the Treason Trial and felt that we had to learn from that and work together.'

In 1956, a year after the ANC and aligned organisations had produced the Freedom Charter as a vision document for a future South Africa, 156 leaders were arrested and charged with high treason. The 'co-conspirators' were mostly former members of the Communist Party of South Africa (which had been banned in 1950), the ANC, the Congress of Democrats and the South African Indian Congress. They included the ANC president-general Chief Albert Luthuli, his deputy Oliver Tambo, Nelson Mandela, Walter Sisulu and many others who would later become celebrated heroes of the liberation struggle. But what attracted Maimane most about the 1956 Treason trialists was the fact that the group was racially mixed.

On Heritage Day, four months after his election as DA leader, Maimane gathered a large group of his supporters outside the derelict Old Synagogue High Court in Pretoria – which is where the Treason Trial had mostly taken place between 1956 and 1961 – to celebrate the holiday. He described the trial as one of the 'pivotal moments in the anti-apartheid struggle', as it 'had consequences that the apartheid government did not foresee':

'Without realising it, the apartheid government had succeeded in bringing together the largest gathering of struggle leaders ever assembled ... They had aided the beginning of a coalition of the willing, a coalition towards change, a coalition of anti-apartheid movements.

'This was not a coalition of black leaders but South Africans from all walks of life. The 156 accused included black, Indian, white and coloured leaders in numbers that reflected the country's diversity.'[31]

Maimane neglects to mention that this 'coalition' had come together long before the Treason Trial. Many of the organisations and leaders involved were already working together by the start of the 1952 Defiance Campaign. It was actually precisely because they had united across racial lines that they were able, despite harassment from the state, to start a nationwide consultative conference that resulted in the adoption of the Freedom Charter by the Congress of the People in Kliptown a year before the trial started.

Despite ample historical evidence that the 'co-conspirators' were comrades-in-arms long before the trial, Maimane inexplicably told his audience that 'in the course of the trial, they discovered that they shared this dream with many people who didn't look exactly like them or speak their language ...'

Without doubt the 1956 Treason Trial was an important milestone in the struggle for liberation, but it certainly didn't mark the start of a non-racial approach to the fight against apartheid, as Maimane seems to suggest. It is this tendency to twist certain historical facts to suit the party's immediate message that often lands the DA and its leaders in trouble with potential voters who regard this as deliberately opportunistic and insincere.

• • •

When Ollis speaks about the 'other people' that Maimane consulted before deciding to join, he does not just mean DA members and its sympathisers. He is also referring to the party's political opponents. In one interview, Maimane has also spoken about having had dialogues with people from Cosatu and even the ANC before he decided on his political path.[32]

Shole-Mashao does not remember the year, but said he recalls a time Maimane told him he was keen on formally joining the ANC. He advised him to find the party branch nearest to him. But Maimane hit a brick wall and later complained to Shole-Mashao about 'gate-keepers' at ANC branch level who 'made him feel like an outsider' partly because his English accent suggested he did not matriculate at a township school.[33]

This sense of alienation, however, would not have been the only reason he drifted away from the ANC. Around 2009, as the general election that would eventually see Zuma's election as president approached, Maimane began speaking favourably to Shole-Mashao about the Congress of the People, a party formed by former defence minister Mosiuoa Lekota and ex-Gauteng premier Mbhazima Shilowa as a breakaway from the ANC in protest against Mbeki's axing from office. He however never actually joined Cope, scared off – as were many like-minded people – by the infighting that characterised the party soon after it became the country's third biggest political party in the National Assembly.

Maimane's emotional ties to the ANC appear to have been further loosened during his time as a master's in Public Administration student at Wits University. The studies, he has said, made him question the ANC's macro-economic policies. He told *Noseweek* that his interest in formal politics only developed while studying towards the MA, and credited one of his professors, Mohammed Jahed, for sparking his interest in politics.[34]

But in the weeks leading up to his historic election as the DA's first black leader, Maimane told members of his Liberty Church[35] a different version of how he got into politics. In the sermon, first brought to the public's attention by DA-strategist-turned-journalist – and Maimane's fiercest critic – Gareth van Onselen, the DA leader strongly suggests that his foray into politics was a calling from God. In a video of the sermon, Maimane addresses the congregation in his capacity as a church elder and lay preacher.

'How I got involved,' he begins the story, 'I was at a church, I was preaching to a community ... and I felt the Lord say to me there is a young person in here ... "you have neglected your political calling". I just felt ... I needed to call this young person to pray for them not to neglect their calling in God.'

In most Pentecostal Churches, the person for whom the holy message was meant would be expected to be so touched by the word that they would stand up or identify themselves by raising their hand so that the pastor could pray with them. Maimane expected the same in this instance, but, he says, 'Just like you are doing now, no one responded. Everybody was like "what is he talking about?" And in a desperate moment you start to ask if anyone has a headache, let's pray for them. There is always a good chance somebody has a headache.'

As he left the church later, Maimane was still perplexed by the prophetic message that no one in the audience responded to. He wondered what had gone wrong. His wife Natalie was with him as he drove back home, worried: 'And when we were in the car, my wife looked at me and said "I think that young person was you."'

Although he was sceptical at first, her words 'planted the seed', Maimane tells the congregation in the video. It took a while, but finally he became convinced that the message was meant for him. The two of them then decided that Maimane, who already had a master's degree in Theology from Bangor University in Wales, would go and study Public Administration in preparation for his new calling.

In another sermon, delivered at a Liberty Church campus in the United Kingdom just two months before his election as Zille's successor, Maimane says this prophesy was revealed 'ten years ago' – suggesting that it would have been in 2005. He states in the sermon that before his 'calling' was prophetically revealed to him, he had no interest in public life: 'It was on the basis of the word,' Maimane testifies to the congregation, that he entered formal politics. 'On that day it was a ridiculous thought, yet God knew the end from the beginning. I still don't know where God is gonna take us ...'[36]

Not long after Maimane had returned from this UK trip, Zille made the announcement that she would not be seeking another term as DA federal leader at the party's next federal congress in May 2015. Her announcement caught Maimane's would-be rivals for the job off-guard, thus helping to smooth his march to the DA throne. Was his a divine anointment? The worshippers who listened to the two sermons reported above might be forgiven for believing so. But for 'liberal purists' who believe politics and religion to be a toxic mix that should never be encouraged, Maimane's suggestion that he had been called by God to enter politics rings alarm bells. If the version

Maimane told to the two churches about how he got involved in politics is the correct one, it would mean that he had long decided – or been anointed – to take up politics as a career when he met Ollis.

Seen from this perspective, his long delay in taking up the DA membership may have been more to do with concerns over which party would best help him attain his ambition than his uneasiness with DA policy positions in a number of areas. In his discussions with Ollis before signing up, Maimane had shown interest in the workings of the country's electoral system as well as how each party gets its members elected into public office.[37]

If indeed he was shopping around for the party that would best serve his public office ambitions, it is no surprise that Maimane found the ANC and its allied organisations unappetising. Had he joined the ANC, the most he could have hoped for would have been to be elected into an ANC Youth League structure,[38] even then, at branch or sub-regional level. The ruling party is not just too big to allow for talented newcomers to immediately shine through, it is a party so steeped in history that – in most cases – one needs to have served it for a decade just to make it as a backbencher on its National Executive Committee.

In contrast, the DA's approach to leadership development puts less emphasis on experience and more on potential talent and skills. Lindiwe Mazibuko, Maimane's predecessor as Leader of the Official Opposition in Parliament, had been with the party for two years when she took over the position in 2009.[39]

And this is not a recent phenomenon. Raenette Taljaard was a master's student in 1996 when she spotted an advert in a newspaper inviting applications from people interested in working as researchers in Parliament. After submitting her CV, she was told she got the job and all she needed was to choose one of the political parties represented in Parliament. She chose the DA's predecessor, the Democratic Party. Three years later, she was that party's Member of Parliament.[40]

A CHANCE ENCOUNTER

The ANC's over-reliance on struggle credentials has left it with most of its key leaders on the wrong side of 50 while its closest rivals – in the form of the DA and the Economic Freedom Fighters – are led by individuals who could still qualify as members of its youth wing. In a country with a young population, this could stand the opposition in good stead for future elections.

But what did Ollis see in Maimane that made him wait so patiently for him to come on board? Perhaps it was the personal friendship that had developed between them. Maimane had even brought a heavily pregnant Natalie over to Ollis's house for a visit. Ollis admits that the personal relationship helped, but also points out that he is a seasoned recruiter who can count up to seven current MPs who came to the party through him. Among them are Gordon Mackay, Patrick Atkinson and Dr Heinrich Volmink: 'It is something I do as a politician,' he says. 'I look for talent. Sometimes I recruit someone and they don't turn out to be the best and sometimes they become a member of Parliament.'

With Maimane, Ollis was convinced that he would be a success because he is 'a people's person' who gets on well with others: 'He is positive and you can see he is a leader because he has a history of leading in churches and NGOs'. (Before politics, one of Maimane's many roles was to lead an NGO called Hope SA.) 'When he came to us he didn't have political experience, but he did have life experience. There is that warmth that you get. He is easy going, easy to talk to and also ethical.'[41]

• • •

It did not take long after Maimane joined the party as a member in the Sandton area – Ollis's constituency – for others to notice his potential. Early in 2011, as the DA was preparing for the local government elections, he decided to make himself available as a candidate for one of the wards in the suburbs of western Johannesburg. Like all other prospective DA election candidates, he was called in for interviews. Apparently he was so good in the interviews that members of the electoral college contacted Helen Zille and said 'we got a guy here who we think is excellent and you have to talk to him about his future career'.[42]

'People marked him then already, saying this one is going to go far,' said Ollis.

Soon after meeting Zille, Maimane was elected the DA's mayoral candidate for Johannesburg. He beat a relatively more experienced Johannesburg DA councillor, Vasco da Gama, in an internal election for the post.

Ollis believes that the DA went for Maimane instead of more experienced councillors in the DA caucus as a mayoral candidate because he had leadership experience from the church. 'Out of all the candidates, he was new. But they felt, you know, he has got qualifications – two master's degrees – and he has run his own business and he has community experience in church. So they felt he would have the ability to speak to people and to run the caucus.'

It soon became clear that the party bosses had earmarked Maimane for far greater things in future: 'In many ways Mmusi Maimane symbolises our party's future,' Zille said glowingly in a statement announcing his mayoral candidacy. 'He is a young, supremely talented individual, committed to the values and principles which define the DA's vision of an Open Opportunity Society for all. He grew up in Soweto, his parents still stay there, and he has lived there most of his life. We welcomed him into the DA and through his own achievement and ability he quickly established himself as a strong emerging leader.'[43]

• • •

Maimane did not win Johannesburg for the DA as he had promised during his campaign that year, but, as he proudly states in his official curriculum vitae, the party did grow its vote base to 34.62 per cent in 2011, from 27.19 per cent in 2006. Ollis believes that, having recognised Maimane's potential, Zille and other party leaders had decided to throw him into the deep end to see if he would sink or swim. His critics, however, doubt if the growth had anything to do with the fact that he was a mayoral candidate, as it was in line with what was happening in other major centres in Gauteng where the DA increased its share of the vote. In Tshwane, for instance, the DA grew by roughly the same margin despite the party's candidate for mayor in the capital city having been Brandon Topham, a local politician with no real public profile.

In his widely circulated and highly critical column, in which he labels Maimane the 'Hollow Man' of South African politics,[44] Gareth van Onselen takes issue with the fact that even though Maimane lost the race for mayorship, he continued to be rewarded with more positions of responsibility in the party. But Ollis counters this by pointing out that it was the DA caucus in the City of Johannesburg, and not party leaders, that elected Maimane as the caucus leader after the 2011 elections: 'All the councillors of the DA in Johannesburg had to vote and choose who they wanted to lead the caucus; they voted for Maimane. And that was a caucus of 90 people,' he says.

One of Van Onselen's most devastating charges against Maimane's rapid rise to the DA's top job, which he believes is undeserved, is that he had a dismal record in his first job as a public representative: 'In three years as leader of arguably the most important metro opposition caucus in the country, he failed to achieve anything of real significance. Certainly he left no indelible mark.'[45]

But Ollis, who had served as a member of the DA caucus in Johannesburg before being promoted to the national Parliament, disagrees. He had long left local government politics when Maimane became caucus leader, but he kept a keen eye on what was happening in the city. 'His first job was a difficult one as he had to lead a team of 90 people and at that stage he had limited experience. That was tough but he did an okay job there and I think that is what gave people confidence that he would achieve something,' Ollis says.[46]

Had Maimane failed, he argues, he would not have been promoted further: 'I think that his years as the DA leader of caucus were the testing ground to see whether or not he was going to make it. Before then, people could see potential, but it was not certain as he had not been in politics for long.'

Zille was clearly impressed. In a matter of months, she appointed Maimane her spokesman. The post was previously held by Lindiwe Mazibuko before her graduation to party leader in Parliament. Seeing that Zille had also been party spokeswoman before she took over from Leon, it was clear that Maimane was being positioned for greater things in future. But it was not always smooth sailing. Newspaper reports began emerging about divisions in the caucus. Some DA councillors privately criticised Maimane for being a novice politician who did not know how to keep them united and focused on holding the ANC-led municipality to account. There were also allegations that he was struggling to manage his different roles, sometimes neglecting caucus in favour of his spokesman duties.

A DA councillor who served under Maimane, but who declined to be named, blamed some of the discontent on members who had not accepted that the newcomer was now their boss: 'He had his mistakes, yes. But some of the complaints were as a result of bitterness, mostly from guys who had been in the party for years only to have this newcomer being put in charge.'

For Ollis, the ructions were part of the hustle and bustle of caucus politics: 'To be caucus leader you have to be elected ... You have to get people to vote for you and then, when they are not doing their job, you have to discipline them. That is very tricky in politics.'[47]

A CHANCE ENCOUNTER

Maimane's 2011 campaign, a mere year after joining the DA, may not have made much of an impact at the polls, but it did launch his public career in a way that many other wet-behind-the ears politicians could only hope for.

His arrival on the Johannesburg local government scene did not dramatically alter people's voting patterns: election results showed that the ANC still enjoyed a large chunk of township and informal settlement votes, while the DA was strong in formerly whites-only suburbs and other areas dominated by minorities. But it did change the way the DA campaigned in traditional ANC strongholds. For the first time in years, when the party's mayoral candidate entered a township, he acted and sounded like the locals and not some outsider who came once every five years canvassing for votes.

CHAPTER 2

An ordinary kasie *boy*

Thabo Shole-Mashao started school a few days later than the other pupils. On his first day at St Angela's Primary School, his teacher, Sister Christine Obotseng – by all accounts a strict disciplinarian who was feared and loved in equal measure by the entire school population – decided to put her Grade 1 class to a test.[1] She instructed the children to write down the numerical figure 1 on their exercise books. Shole-Mashao did not know how to write at all. But sitting next to him was a taller boy who seemed to be an old hand in what, to Shole-Mashao, was still a new world of writing and reading numbers and letters.

The young Shole-Mashao watched in despair as the other boy effortlessly did as the teacher had instructed. He must have looked really desperate, because, without uttering a word, the other boy quickly took the exercise book and scribbled the figure for him.

On seeing her new pupil's effort, with the number written down so well, as if by a hand that had practised it several times before, Sister Christine became suspicious. Who had done the work for him, she demanded to know. Frightened, Shole-Mashao pointed to the boy sitting next to him, who he would soon know as Mmusi Aloysias Maimane. The memory is still fresh: 'The teacher scolded him. He got into big trouble for helping me.'[2]

And so began a lifetime of great friendship between these two boys from Dobsonville Township, a blacks-only settlement established by the apartheid government to supply cheap labour for Roodepoort, on the West Rand, and the greater Johannesburg area.

When the young Maimane and Shole-Mashao started school in the mid-1980s, the apartheid system was already creaking, facing rejection and condemnation both at home and abroad. Years later, two decades after apartheid had fallen, one of the boys would rise to become the first black leader of a party with deep roots in the whites-only political system. The other would be a prominent figure in radio and television broadcasting, working as a producer, talk-show host and entrepreneur.

Shole-Mashao tells the story of how their friendship began to make a point about what he sees as Maimane's greatest attribute – his natural kindness and inclination to help those in need. It is a quality that many of those who have known Maimane since his childhood and as a pupil at St Angela's or *eRoma* – the name Dobsonville residents prefer for the independent school on Mayikani Street – never fail to remark on. Some even suggest that he was 'too much of a nice guy'[3] to suspect that he would be in the dog-eat-dog world of politics some day, not to mention be the main leader of a party whose immediate mission is to aggressively challenge the continent's oldest liberation movement's political dominance in the country.

A week before his election as DA leader, the *Sunday Times* dubbed Maimane 'the Soweto nice guy' who would be DA king.[4]

On meeting Maimane in person, it is not difficult to see why the 'nice guy' label has stuck. Always warm and courteous, even when interacting with his political rivals, there is an air of sincerity about him that is often lacking in most politicians. His childhood friends attribute this to his upbringing as well as his strong religious beliefs.

Maimane was born on Friday, 6 June 1980, at the Leratong Hospital[5] – a Krugersdorp health facility reserved for blacks in terms of the apartheid segregation policies of the time. It was his paternal grandmother who gave him the name Mmusi, which means governor or leader in seTswana. His second name, Aloysias, came from his maternal grandmother, who wished he would one day grow to be a church leader[6] – a dream Maimane later fulfilled.

He is the first of four children born to Simon and Ethel Maimane.[7] His parents were migrants who met and fell in love in the then Transvaal some three years before Maimane was born. Simon, a Motswana from the Bafokeng clan, had left the then Bophuthatswana Bantustan – now part of modern-day North West province – 'landless and jobless'[8] and settled in Kagiso township on the West Rand. His mother Ethel hails from Cofimvaba in the former Transkei, birthplace of struggle hero Chris Hani. She grew up in a poor rural household she shared with her parents and six siblings.[9] When she was old enough, she left the Eastern Cape for Johannesburg in the hope of better employment prospects in the future.

Maimane is very proud of his mixed ethnic heritage and, like his proficiency in seven official languages and mixed marriage, he is not shy to use it to convince would-be voters that he is the quintessential Rainbow Nation leader, not just representative of one specific South African language group.

Delivering his first speech as the new DA leader at the party's sixth federal congress in May 2015 in Port Elizabeth, Maimane began by describing the Eastern Cape as his ancestral home: '*Ndizalwa yintombi yakwaMaduna, ooGubevu, OoTiba kumandla waseCofimvaba* – I am of a daughter of the Madunas, the Gubevus, the Tibas from the district of Cofimvaba.'[10]

It is not usual in many of our cultures that a person introduces themselves by singing their maternal clan names, but Maimane has done so several times when touring the Eastern Cape[11] as a way of convincing local voters that he is partly one of their own. And his Eastern Cape audiences love it. They cheered wildly and ululated as Maimane chanted his mother's clan names at the party's Safe City Rally at Gelvandale Stadium, in the gang-infested northern suburbs of Port Elizabeth in November of that year.

Earlier that day, beaming with pride, Maimane had shown me pictures of himself and some of his uncles that he had taken on his phone during DA campaign rallies in Cofimvaba and Butterworth. He was pleased by the turnout at both events, to him a sign that – under him – the DA was making inroads in a province that was historically regarded as solid ANC territory. 'We would not even go to Butterworth in the past,' he said as he scrolled from the selfies he had taken with his relatives to more general pictures of hundreds of supporters in blue DA T-shirts.

However neither the former Transkei nor Lucas Mangope's Bophuthatswana played any significant part in Maimane's life as a youngster. His friends describe the young Mmusi as having been a typical township boy who spent his afternoons after school doing his house chores and then playing football in the streets and the local soccer field before heading home just before dark to do his homework.

Although he went to an independent primary school, his parents were by no means rich. St Angela's was one of the schools established by the Church in the 1960s and 1970s to cater for African children following the introduction of legislation that prohibited the existence of racially mixed schools.

Mission schools had suffered a major blow in 1954 when the Nationalist government – which had come to power six years earlier on a ticket of imposing the apartheid system in the country – passed into law the Bantu Education Act which condemned blacks to an inferior education system. Explaining the new law, which brought all schools that taught Africans under direct national government control, the minister of native affairs, Dr

HF Verwoerd, said the Act was aimed at 'transforming education for Natives into Bantu Education'.

He spelt it out: 'By blindly producing pupils trained on a European model, the vain hope was created among Natives that they could occupy posts within the European community despite the country's policy of Apartheid. This is what is meant by the creation of "unhealthy white collar ideals" and the causation of widespread frustration among the so-called educated Natives ... The school must equip him to meet the demands which the economic life of South Africa will impose on him. There is no place for him in the European community above the levels of certain forms of labour.'[12]

Out of fear that the new legislation, together with the Group Areas Act and other segregationist policies, could result in its missionaries – most of whom were white and European – being banned from working in the townships, the Catholic Church established the Companions of Saint Angela Merici, which comprised mainly black nuns and operated in the Johannesburg region. The Companions of Saint Angela Merici considered school as important in spreading their faith and believed that their work in education also helped 'to raise the status of woman and enhance her dignity in the world of today'.[13] St Angela's became one of the schools that the sisters used to advance their progressive ideas in spite of government's attempt to use the education system to subjugate the majority of the population.

In 1976, four years before Maimane was born, opposition to the apartheid education system – especially the insistence by the government that Afrikaans was to be the language of instruction in township schools – led to mass student revolts in Soweto and the surrounding areas. The violence, which began on 16 June, when police opened fire on protesting students, claimed hundreds of lives and thousands of injuries. It caused hundreds of Soweto youth to skip the country and join the banned ANC, PAC and other liberation struggle organisations. According to the National Party government's Cillie Commission of Enquiry into the uprising, 576 people died in the clashes – 451 of them killed by the police – and 3 907 suffered injuries (figures rejected as too low by representatives of the affected families).[14]

According to Maimane, his mother Ethel was among those who 'ran through the streets of Soweto in the protests of '76: 'She did it because she knew that this was a cause worth fighting for. She was fighting for black liberation, for better education for blacks.'[15] It is no surprise therefore that when their first-born child was old enough to start school, Ethel and her husband sought 'better education' for him by sending him to St Angela's. That they were both devout Catholics and that the school was a few blocks away from their modest house on Dobsonville's Mmutle Street would have played no small part in the decision.

Ethel worked as a cashier at a Hyperama while her husband, Simon, was a factory worker at a company that produced gas cylinders.[16] Simon supplemented his meagre blue-collar worker salary by running a mini-shebeen at his house. The drinking spot catered only for a mature clientele that appreciated good music. As a result, Maimane senior was one of the most popular figures in the neighbourhood and locals say his love for soul music remains legendary.[17]

Maimane describes his father as 'what I call a high relater' who 'knows everybody in Dobsonville'.[18] His father, he says, never discriminated against anyone in their neighbourhood and was 'always accessible' to everyone.[19] It is a trait the young Maimane, say his neighbours, has inherited from his father. Whenever he is in Dobsonville to see his parents and his siblings – sisters Cecelia and Tumelo as well as brother Kabelo – Maimane does not leave without first walking around the neighbourhood checking up on friends and old acquaintances.

Among those who frequented his father's shebeen and became a close family friend of the Maimanes was 1980s superstar band Stimela's founder member, keyboardist and songwriter Thapelo Khomo. Other members of this popular group, which won many hearts and minds by using music to protest against racial discrimination and oppression, would occasionally accompany Khomo to see the older Maimane.

Kgotla Molefe, whose own home is not far from the Maimanes', remembers being chased away, along with other children, as they stood outside the yard to get a glimpse of these men whose voices and faces were always on radio and television. 'Even though they sold alcohol, they were very strict,' he remembers. 'They did not want any children around when the elders were doing their thing.' They applied even stricter discipline when it came to their son, Molefe says: 'Everything had its time with him. They taught him balance. He would play with us and then go home when it was time for books.'[20]

But, as the African saying goes, it takes a village to raise a child. So Maimane's parents were not the only ones responsible for his upbringing. Many others within his extended family and neighbourhood played their parts.

The one person beside his parents who seems to have had the greatest influence on him as a child was his father's aunt, Lilian Morake – mother to Bafana Bafana spokesman and former SABC sports journalist Matlhomola Morake. In interviews, Maimane says Lilian Morake was a 'devout, disciplined woman' who taught him that 'all you really have in life is your own principles and convictions'.[21] She also impressed upon him the values of ubuntu and respect for others, especially those who are much older than you. These are the values he still lives by, he says, even though at times they seem to be at odds with his political role. For instance, Maimane confesses that one of the toughest decisions he had to make as a leader of the DA in Parliament was how to address President Jacob Zuma – a man 'who is old enough to be my grandfather'.[22] 'I have never addressed him as just Jacob Zuma; it's President Zuma. It is about showing respect. There are cultural difficulties.'[23]

A few years before he took up politics as a career, Maimane was a regular blogger for TomorrowToday Global, a change management consultancy specialising in business leadership development and motivational speaking. In one of his blogs for the company's website, Maimane says his upbringing was 'a message that everyone who is older than you is your father and mother':

'It was that if an older person was in the room you had to stand to greet them; if you were in a bus and they came through, you'd offer up your seat; it was that you address them by their title or, at the very least, add a prefix to their name – Bra so and so or Mr Sibanibani (so and so) and *Ubaba ka Sibanibani* (father of so and so).'[24]

Maimane's attitude towards 'respect' for one's 'elders' in the political arena is in direct contrast to that of his main competitors on the opposition benches – the Economic Freedom Fighters. When National Assembly Speaker Baleka Mbete took issue with the way the EFF's second-in-charge, Floyd Shivambu, addressed her during a sitting in late 2004, she told him she was 'not your peer' and therefore expected him to treat her as his elder:

'You are an African child, brought up by people I respect and I'm quite sure you're not reflecting the way you were brought up,' said 65-year-old Mbete to Shivambu, who is 31 years her junior.

'What are you talking about? This is a professional relationship ... You're not my mother. I'm here as a Member of Parliament,' retorted Shivambu.[25]

For Maimane, the Shivambu response would have been unthinkable. Even in his most devastating speech in Parliament, in which he called Zuma a 'broken man', Maimane says he was always careful to strike a balance between expressing his frustration with the President's refusal to appear and account to Parliament and showing respect for him.

Most notably, Maimane's take on politics and 'respect for the elders' also differs sharply from the approach that had been taken by his predecessor as Leader of the Opposition in Parliament, Lindiwe Mazibuko.

Mazibuko, who often came under fire from ANC MPs for allegedly showing little regard for Zuma's status as President as well as her elder, told a newspaper that: 'You earn respect by delivering to the people and by conducting yourself with integrity ... It is not good in a democratic society to go around demanding respect. You must earn respect.'[26]

But can Maimane's approach, especially in a parliament that has become increasingly acrimonious, especially due to the arrival of the EFF and the ANC's over-reliance on its numerical strength rather than political persuasion, be put down simply to the way he was brought up or his natural predisposition to avoid a dirty fight?

Kgotla Molefe recalls that as young boys, if anyone challenged Alu – Maimane's nickname, which was derived from his 'school name' Aloysias – to a fight, 'he would just walk home without a fight'.[27] At school, Alu feared corporal punishment so much that Shole-Mashao says he would try to negotiate himself out of trouble with the teacher whenever he was in trouble. Molefe also remembers Alu as being close to his sister Cecelia, so close that whenever his parents gave Maimane a hiding for doing wrong, Cecelia would cry with him.

All of this, I suggested to Molefe, painted a picture of a young Maimane as what other kids in the streets would term a 'softie', a 'mama's boy' or, to borrow from township lingo, 'a cheeseboy'.

'Never! He never was a cheeseboy. He was an ordinary *kasie* [township] boy, it is just that he came from a home that valued discipline,' Molefe answered.

There is another possible explanation: his religious beliefs. As we will see later in this chapter, the church was an important part of Maimane's life. In interviews he has intimated that, as a young boy, the eight Beatitudes Jesus Christ gave in his Sermon on the Mount left a big impression on him: 'The idea of "blessed are the peacemakers". This was drilled into us as kids, at school and at church. I thought if there was one ambition to have, it was to become a peacemaker.'[28]

If the young Maimane loathed physical violence, it does not mean that he was not fiercely competitive. Even though they were the best of friends, Shole-Mashao says there was always competition between them over who would get higher marks than the other. The two were apparently always in the top five of their class's best pupils.

This competitive spirit was also visible on the soccer field. Both Molefe and Shole-Mashao say Maimane was mad about soccer as a child, and they describe him as an above-average midfielder when he played for an amateur club, Ontario, which was based in the section of the township called Long Till. At school during lunch break, Shole-Mashao says, they would play football. Even after school, they would seldom leave the premises without playing a quick game. When they were doing Standard 4 (which is now known as Grade 6), a teacher discovered an exercise book among Maimane's belongings in which he had copied down the full fixture list of all the professional National Soccer League games for that season.

From a young age Maimane supported Kaizer Chiefs, the soccer team that dominated local football and produced the most soccer stars in the 1970s and for most of the 1980s. Among the Chiefs legends whose pictures he would use to decorate his school books were the likes of Marks 'Go Man Go' Maponyane, Howard Freeze and Ntsie Maphike.[29] But it was Theophilus Doctor Khumalo he loved the most. On the soccer field, whenever he had the ball, he would start doing commentary, mimicking a radio commentator, and would refer to himself as '16V', one of the nicknames the Kaizer Chiefs and soccer national team star was known by.

'I really thought he would grow up to become a soccer commentator. He used to love doing commentary, he loved football,' said Molefe.

Soccer is still very much part of Maimane's life, even though he is no longer actively involved. Often during summer holidays, he takes time off to watch amateur football tournaments in Dobsonville.[30] When Dobsonville Stadium was the home ground for the then Premier Soccer League outfit, Moroka Swallows, Maimane would often be seen at the venue, especially when Swallows played Kaizer Chiefs.

In the English premiership, Maimane favours Liverpool Football Club.

His affection for the game often shines through when addressing the party faithful at political rallies and protest marches. For instance, when the Supreme Court of Appeal ruled in the DA's favour in a court case against the SABC and its controversial Chief Operations Officer, Hlaudi Motsoeneng, Maimane used a soccer analogy to explain the significance of the ruling: 'It's like soccer this thing. It has quarter-finals and semi-finals and finally, a final. At the quarter-finals we took Hlaudi to the Western Cape High Court and we beat him there.'[31] Now that Motsoeneng had lost in his 'semi-final' bid at the SCA to have a ruling that he be removed from his post overturned, continued Maimane, the DA was readying itself for the final against Zuma. By the 'final', he was referring to the DA's Constitutional Court case to compel Zuma to comply with the recommendations of Public Protector Thuli Madonsela that he pay back a portion of the R246-million spent on his private residence in Nkandla.

However, Maimane's passion for sport was not limited to football. As he grew older and became exposed to other sporting codes, he would come back home and try to introduce those 'new' sports to his neighbourhood friends. At Allen Glen High School, the multi-racial school he attended in Roodepoort, he developed a strong attachment to tennis. He would arrive in the township from school carrying tennis rackets and balls with him and would teach his peers to play the sport.[32] They would draw up lines on the road, transforming Mlotywa Street into a makeshift tennis court.

At school Maimane also grew to be a rugby fan (he often names the Gauteng

Lions as his favourite team). He introduced volleyball in the area and was known to also be a cricket enthusiast. 'I guess those were the first signs of leadership,' said Molefe. 'He introduced us to a lot of sports that were not being played in this township. He brought a lot of new things, now he is bringing the DA. That too was new here as most people had always been ANC.'

• • •

The story of the young Maimane would not be complete without talking about religion, for that played a central part in his growth to becoming the politician he is today. Raised by dedicated Catholic parents, he was active in church activities at a very young age. Fikile-Ntsikelelo Moya, who was Maimane's senior when they were altar boys at St Angela's Catholic Church, remembers him as a 'quiet and intelligent' youngster who got himself actively involved in church activities. He went beyond his duty as an altar boy, even starting his own junior liturgy class for fellow Sunday school children at the church. 'He was leading us, he would call us to meetings that lasted for hours. Sometimes we would start at 11 am and finish at 7 pm,' recalls Shole-Mashao.

By the time he was in Standard 5, Maimane was a conscientious Catholic who many in his community believed would grow up to play an important role in the church. It therefore came as a surprise to many of his peers and friends when he suddenly left the church of his parents, broader family and close friends to join what Moya calls a 'more bible-based church'. The transformation appears to have happened in his mid-teens when he started attending Saturday classes and Christianity-based youth camps.

Maimane had been selected to be part of a group of scholars who did extra lessons in English, mathematics and science at Pace Commercial Secondary School in Jabulani every Saturday. Pace was regarded as one of the better educational institutions in the township, having been established as part of a joint initiative by local and American business communities in 1981 as a specialist school in commercial subjects. To be selected for the weekend extra classes at the school invariably meant that you were performing above average and the teachers believed you had a great future ahead of you.

Maimane regards his selection to participate in those classes as a life-changing experience, as it opened new doors of opportunity for him. He told the *Sowetan* in October 2012 that two white teachers, Alec and Linda Galanakis, who ran the Saturday school, were 'key in my getting a quality education'.[33]

Shole-Mashao and Molefe said it was during this period that Maimane became exposed to the Evangelical Student Christian Movement and religious youth movements. He became so deeply involved and committed to his new faith that, according to Molefe, he would insist that every meeting or communal gathering they attended started and ended with a prayer. He still played soccer, all right, but never on a Sunday.

The young Maimane's decision to change denominations would have come as a great shock to his parents, but they supported him in his decision, as they would do later when he chose to change his political allegiance from the ANC to the DA. However – though they changed their preferred political party to back him – his parents and siblings remain active Catholics. His father sings in the church choir and Cecelia, his sister, is often involved with organising liturgical activities at the church.[34]

That Maimane decided to convert to another denomination so early in life, at a time when he was still largely dependent on his parents for school, food and general upkeep, indicates an independence and courage to stand up for what he believes in, no matter the possible consequences.

It was through his involvement with Pace College that Maimane later got to be a pupil at Allen Glen High School, a mixed-race public school established in Weltevreden Park, Roodepoort, just before the end of formal apartheid in 1993. One of his teachers at Pace College, Alec Galanakis, taught history at the new school. Speaking at the school's twenty-first birthday celebration ceremony in October 2014, Maimane told the audience that it was at the school that he honed his leadership skills. 'I was a prefect and also served on the school's governing body,' he said, 'where I learned how to lead and deal with the challenges that come with leadership.'[35]

It was as a pupil at the school that Maimane began 'commuting between two worlds'[36] – one white and the other black. 'I'd get to this white school and I was called Aloysias because it was just easier. Then I'd get home and my parents called me Mmusi. So I lived in these dual worlds. I didn't rank them and I was quite fine with both names.'[37]

Did this 'dual worlds' existence develop in him what renowned twentieth-century African American scholar WEB Du Bois termed 'double-consciousness', which he defined as 'this sense of always looking at one's self through the eyes of others, of measuring one's soul by the tape of a world that looks on in amused contempt and pity'?[38]

His friend Shole-Mashao appears to have believed so when both of them were still at high school. The two had separated and gone to different schools after Standard 5. While Maimane immersed himself in his studies, church and sports, Shole-Mashao mixed academic studies with student politics. He used to be frustrated by the failure of Maimane and other peers at their 'Model C' – that is, relatively privileged[39] – school to get involved in the high school student struggles of the time.

A Black Consciousness Movement adherent at the time, Shole-Mashao believed that Maimane's exposure 'to the other side' through school and other 'extra-racial activities' had made him 'too accommodating'.[40] For Maimane, however, the focus was primarily on doing well in his studies. He got to Allen Glen through a bursary and knew that, on their own, his parents would not be able to keep him at the school and still pay for the education of their three other children.

'I didn't grow up with a silver spoon in my mouth. I came from an ordinary home,' he says. 'My father used to say he would go without socks so that I could go to school.'[41]

Maimane had to work at piece jobs during weekends to help his parents feed the family. Even without much money, his parents were determined that their son would achieve what they never did – get a university degree. When he matriculated in 1997, Maimane and his parents could not afford tuition at most of the country's universities. He eventually opted to study via correspondence at the University of South Africa (Unisa), where he later obtained his Psychology degree.

His experience is a typical story for thousands of township and rural youth who pass their matric every year hoping to go to university, only to learn that they are too poor to afford tertiary education. As the #FeesMustFall movement dramatically reminded us at the end of 2015, even those lucky enough to make it through government funding and private sector bursaries are increasingly finding university education too expensive.

Maimane and the DA hope that his personal story of struggle and perseverance will help change the perception of those voters who see the party as too white and elitist.

'My own story and biography has allowed more South Africans to say: "Wait, he understands poverty; he understands not having access to opportunity; he understands discrimination."'[42]

• • •

In 2004, as democratic South Africa celebrated its tenth birthday and the ANC prepared for another resounding victory at the polls, a senior DA official – who later became an influential leader in the party – told a small group of journalists I was with that she believed the ruling party would be out of office by 2019. It was at a DA media function a few months before the elections and the pollsters were predicting a two-thirds majority for the ANC, which it subsequently got. So to us the DA official's predictions sounded too optimistic, if not totally off the mark. But she insisted, telling us that the 'turning point' would be around 2009 when many of the thousands of black children who would have grown up attending Model C schools would be eligible to vote. This generation of voters, she argued, would not be as 'race obsessed' as older generations, as they would have grown up in a school environment where race was not a determining factor of one's success or failure. The DA, she predicted, would be under an entirely different leadership by then – one that was reflective of the party's demographics.

Although the DA official got the last part right – the DA now has a black federal leader and most of its provincial structures are led by black people – it would seem that her faith in 'Model C' black voters was misplaced. For starters, they have proven not to be monolithic – especially when it comes to politics. Secondly, many of them appear to be as race conscious as the generations that come before them – if not even more so.

Given that, by way of background, he shares a lot of life experiences with this category of voters, is Maimane the kind of leader to finally win them over to the DA while at the same time keeping the party's traditional constituencies loyal to it? The party's electoral successes at a number of tertiary institutions since Maimane became DA leader suggest this may be the case. But his rejection by protesting students during the #FeesMustFall campaign at the University of Cape Town, as well as the Democratic Alliance Student Organisation's inability to play any meaningful role during those protests, may suggest that Maimane has not made the kind of impact the party expected when it elected him leader.

CHAPTER 3

....

The Obama of Soweto

TUESDAY AFTERNOON, 17 FEBRUARY 2015: the heatwave predicted by the South African Weather Service hung heavy over Cape Town, while in the cooler air of the National Assembly Mmusi Maimane took the couple of steps from his parliamentary seat to the podium to deliver his most defining speech yet as Leader of the Opposition. Even though the general political atmosphere in the country was heavy with apprehension, no one – except those in Maimane's inner circle – would have predicted that his reply to Zuma's State of the Nation Address would turn up the heat to such a degree.

Five days earlier, South Africa had watched aghast as the National Assembly chamber descended into violence and chaos as police and parliamentary security personnel physically ejected EFF MPs from the House.

The MPs, led by Malema, had continuously disrupted Zuma's State of the Nation Address by demanding that he first tell the country when he planned to pay back some of the money used to upgrade his private home in Nkandla at taxpayers' expense. For the first time in the country's history, police had marched into the hallowed chamber and had used brute force to resolve what was essentially a political disagreement. To make matters worse, in the hours leading up to Parliament's showdown with the EFF, the State Security department had secretly installed a signal jammer in the House – blocking access to mobile phone networks – in a cynical move to prevent journalists from live-tweeting images of the chaos as it unfolded. Democratic South Africa appeared to be headed for a new and dangerous phase: that of a security state.

Moments after EFF MPs were dramatically forced out of the chambers, kicking and screaming, Maimane and the rest of his caucus looked visibly shaken, unsure of their next move. They had all arrived in Parliament dressed in black as a symbol of their 'mourning the death of democracy' under Zuma's rule, but seemed not to have prepared for how violent the confrontation between the EFF and security personnel would turn out to be.

With the EFF out of the picture and Parliament preparing to go ahead with the ceremony as if nothing significant had just happened, it was now up to Maimane to make the next move. Rising on a point of order, he demanded to know from National Assembly Speaker Baleka Mbete and her co-presiding officer, National Council of Provinces chairperson Thandi Modise, if police officers had been among the security people, all dressed in black pants and white shirts, who had stormed into the House to remove the EFF. When he did not get a satisfactory answer, he threatened to lead a DA walkout from the Assembly. But when some of his party's representatives, including Zille, who was in the House in her capacity as Western Cape Premier, stood up to leave, Maimane sat down again, causing confusion. A few minutes later, following a heated exchange of words between DA chief whip John Steenhuisen and Modise, the DA finally staged a walk-out.

In the hours and days that followed, Maimane's critics used the temporary confusion to claim that he had no control over the caucus he led. Steenhuisen rather than Maimane, they alleged, called the shots. Although the DA rejected this allegation, when the next week began Maimane found himself in a fairly weakened position. He needed a strong reply to Zuma's address if he was not to be relegated to the sidelines in what was building up to be a great Malema versus Zuma parliamentary confrontation. The public's attention was hardly on the DA; everybody seemed keen to know what Malema's next move would be. But it did not take long for everyone to pay attention when Maimane's turn finally came to respond to Zuma's State of the Nation Address.

South Africa had allowed a 'powerful man to get away with too much for too long,'[1] went Maimane's opening salvo. 'This honourable man is here in our presence today,' he continued. Turning slightly to his right, he looked Zuma in the eye (the President's parliamentary seat is a couple of metres from the podium): 'Honourable President, in these very chambers, just five days ago, you broke Parliament.'

But just in case Zuma thought Maimane had used 'honourable' as a term of endearment, the DA leader quickly warned him not to take the term literally; he was using it only 'out of respect for the traditions and conventions of this august House'.

And then he turned up the furnace, delivering his devastating and most memorable punch lines: 'For you, honourable President, are not an honourable man. You are a broken man, presiding over a broken society.'

Zuma's roasting had begun. Maimane went on to accuse the President of 'breaking every democratic institution' to avoid facing the courts on charges of corruption. He slammed Zuma for laughing while opposition MPs were being forced out of the House by the police.

The President was stung. But he did not show it at first, completely ignoring Maimane's input when he responded to the State of the Nation debate two days later.[2] It took more than a month for the full extent of his fury over Maimane's speech to make itself felt in full. The occasion was Zuma's appearance before Parliament to answer MPs' questions relating to his executive's performance. But instead of an all-out counterattack on Maimane, Zuma chose to mock him by imitating the DA leader's speech and suggesting that his contribution to parliamentary debates was meaningless.

'You know part of the reason I can't deal with all the contributions ... I am dealing with contributions that were meaningful, because others [sic] there was nothing said: "There is a broken president in a broken ... *Maye babo* [my goodness]!"' Zuma said as he gesticulated and grimaced while the ANC benches roared with laughter.[3]

There is no doubt however that, despite Zuma's attempt at dismissing Maimane's attack on him, the blistering speech won the DA parliamentary leader scores of new fans. He had captured the general political mood in the country, especially among those who were still horrified by the state's high-handed response to the EFF's disruption of the President's address. Maimane's critics within the DA who had questioned the wisdom of electing a political novice to head its 89-member caucus began to accept that he was not the disaster they had feared he would be.

At times during the tempestuous early months of the fifth Parliament, he seemed out of his depth as Leader of the Official Opposition – a constitutionally recognised title that carries with it much responsibility. He was often overshadowed by Malema who, with far fewer MPs, was increasingly setting the agenda in Parliament with his brash and combative brand of politics.

Comparisons between Maimane and his predecessor, Lindiwe Mazibuko, were also becoming unavoidable. During Mazibuko's tenure as Leader of the Opposition, the DA had set the political agenda for other opposition parties in Parliament on such contentious issues as the controversial upgrading of the President's private home in Nkandla. Helped by the fact that with every election the DA registered growth when all other parties were losing votes, its performance in Parliament under Mazibuko enhanced the party's status as the only viable alternative to the governing ANC. But now, with Mazibuko off to study at Harvard and the new kids on the block making their presence felt in the legislature, the DA found itself playing second fiddle to the EFF – at times having to mimic its antics in a desperate attempt not to be overshadowed. That it was the DA, through Mazibuko, that had set the ball rolling when it asked Public Protector Thuli Madonsela to investigate the Nkandla scandal seemed forgotten; the EFF, with its 'Pay Back the Money' slogan, now drove the campaign.

Maimane's encounter with the Nkandla scandal predates his role as an MP. He had taken an interest in the matter in his previous role as the DA's national spokesman and made it one of his campaign issues during his 2014 failed bid to become Gauteng premier.[4] A day after Madonsela released her scathing 'Secure in Comfort' report into how taxpayers' money had been squandered and how Zuma had 'unduly benefited from the enormous capital investment',[5] Maimane flew down to Durban and drove another 188 kilometres to Nkandla where he laid charges of corruption against the President.

It was an overcast morning in Nkandla; KwaNxamalala village, where the Zuma homestead is located, was a hive of activity as heavily armed police and a large media contingent drove up and down the main road in anticipation of trouble. Maimane had widely publicised his planned visit to the area, undeterred by the fact that similar trips by other opposition leaders in the past had ended in heated confrontation with Zuma-supporting villagers. As it turned out, the visit of about 14 party officials and film crew was without any incidents: the handful of ANC supporters who had bothered to show up on the day were kept far from the DA contingent at the police station.

But despite Maimane's outspokenness and his laying of criminal charges over the scandal, Nkandla had become an EFF campaign issue by the beginning of 2015. The DA had long lost the initiative. So when Maimane delivered his 'broken man' speech, he was not just going after Zuma; he had set out to win back the confidence of opposition voters as well as to send out a clear message that he, and not Malema, was the official leader of the opposition in the National Assembly.

Although the content of the speech was important, it was the eloquent and charismatic manner in which he powerfully delivered it that won Maimane many hearts and respect from even his political foes. All the public speaking skills he had acquired over the years, as a keen member of a debating society at school, a preacher at church and a paid public speaker at corporate events, seemed to be at play on the day.

Maimane was to later reveal to journalist Sam Mkokeli that it took him and his four speech-writers hours of practice before getting it right. 'Gosh, I must have read that speech well over 10 times,' he said.[6]

Not many South African politicians regard good speech writing and delivery as essential tools in their trade any more. Though a long tradition of great orators across the racial and political divide kept the country apart for centuries, politics nowadays is dominated by public speakers who go through their speeches as if they were reading a shopping list out aloud. In some cases, the audience could be forgiven for suspecting that the politician is encountering his or her speech for the first time as they disjointedly read each sentence as if it has no connection with the previous one or the one that comes after it.

Maimane's oratory skills, some of which were without doubt sharpened in the pulpit where he spends many of his Sundays preaching to congregants at his church, can be counted among his greatest strengths as a politician. It is partly his ability to hold the audience's attention during a speech that earned him the moniker Obama of Soweto. Even public speaking specialists are impressed: The Voice Clinic's Monique Harrisberg once described Maimane as 'a wonderful speaker' who 'reminds me of US president Barack Obama'.[7]

But rousing speeches were not the only thing going for Obama when he first won over the hearts and minds of mainly young Americans as he began his successful campaign to become the first black president of the United States. His campaign involved the articulation of a clear vision for America and the world, and the propagation of sound policies Obama believed were needed to get the US out of the economic and international relations crisis the country found itself in during George W Bush's eight-year tenure as president.

Maimane lacks that, his critics often complain. He over-relies on his public speaking abilities to conceal the fact that he has no real solutions of his own, they charge. Journalist Jan-Jan Joubert, who has followed the DA for several years and was one of the reporters who broke the story about Zille hastily convening a party leadership meeting in April 2015 to announce her plans to step down, is one of those who hold this opinion of Maimane: 'He is a good public speaker and, as with such speakers, they are only good when they have good speeches in front of them. He does not actually write his own,' he pointed out.[8]

The notion of Maimane as a mere actor playing a character that has already been scripted for him gained currency in political circles in the weeks leading up to his election as new DA leader. Columnist and former DA staffer Gareth van Onselen wrote two searing articles that put into question his suitability for the party's top job. In the first of the two, Van Onselen described Maimane as the DA's own 'Manchurian candidate',[9] hence likening him to a character in a novel and movie by the same name who runs for public office at the behest of his puppet masters. The character has no views of his own and does, for the most part, as he is told.

The subsequent article called Maimane a 'hollow man' who is surrounded by 'the biggest production team the party has ever assembled'. Van Onselen continues: 'Any rare conversation with him on a difficult subject, sans a full and proper briefing, is like watching a news presenter with a broken teleprompter. They might boast a golden voice but the words are incoherent and, ultimately, meaningless.'[10]

Party leaders such as De Lille and Ollis disagree with the claim that Maimane has no ideas of his own and point out that, even before he formally joined the party, he had begun sharing with them ideas on how the opposition to the ANC should work in future.[11] As we will see later in the book, by early 2016 – stung by the racism controversy that had threatened the DA's potential growth among black voters – Maimane had begun to stamp his authority over the party, assertively setting new rules of engagement.

How ironic, however, that he should be likened to a TV presenter who heavily depends on a 'teleprompter' for his lines. For there was a time – long before his forays into politics – when he had to depend on teleprompters and rehearsed scripts for a living. He does not mention it in his official curriculum vitae, but Maimane was once a television presenter on SABC1, the country's most watched channel, doing a Christian magazine programme that was aired on Sunday mornings.

The Crux religious show was a popular programme that mainly catered for viewers between the ages of 18 and 30. SABC viewership figures at the time indicated that the show was watched by about 800 000 viewers every Sunday.[12] Maimane joined Crux in the mid-2000s and, according to those who worked with him at the show, soon proved himself to be a natural.

David Seletisha, who produced the show at the time, remembers Maimane as a conscientious presenter who would not go in front of a camera without thoroughly rehearsing the script first. 'There was no lazy day for him,' he says, 'and he did not have a lot of re-takes when filming. He was always on point, as he was one of those guys who always wanted to check the script before recording started ... Once the camera was on him, you could see ... My feeling was always that the guy was made for TV.'[13]

Seletisha expected Maimane to one day graduate into acting. It was not an unreasonable expectation: Crux presenters such as the late Precious Simelane, Andrew Webster, Kim Adams and Thokozani Nkosi ended up having successful television careers. It took him by surprise to learn that, instead of venturing into movie making, Maimane had chosen a life in politics: 'He never spoke politics but showed keen interest in NGOs.'

At work, Maimane came across to colleagues as reserved, almost to the point of shyness, recalled Seletisha: 'You had to talk to him before he would open up to you. He takes time to warm up to you and it took me a few months before I got to know him well. If you don't know him that much you would think that he is aloof.' He never brought his friends to the recordings and, according to Seletisha, only came with his wife Natalie 'once or twice' to the show.

Crux was to be the only TV programme in which Maimane was in front of the camera as a presenter, but it was not his only involvement with the medium. In 2006, he was actively involved with Heartlines, a Christian-orientated NGO that produced eight TV drama films for SABC 2.[14]

Heartlines, which won several awards for the films, describes itself on its website as a 'God-inspired initiative aimed at promoting values-based transformation in South Africa and beyond'. The dramas, which were released under the theme '8 Weeks – 8 Values – One National Conversation' focused on such issues as HIV/Aids, corruption, reconciliation and how to save money.[15] Here Maimane's role was behind the scenes, mostly assisting with the formulation of discussion notes for church groups and youth formations on issues arising from the films.

Years later, the DA would use Maimane's television experience to its advantage. As the date for the 2014 general election drew near, the party intensified its drive for votes by launching two television ad campaigns. The first, which came out in March of that year, was shot in Nkandla on the very day the Public Protector released her final report on the gross wastage of taxpayers' money at the homestead. It had Maimane standing in front of the KwaNxamalala village police station with Zuma's sprawling property in the background, asking: 'How could they allow millions to be spent on one man while so many are suffering? What has happened to the ANC? The ANC has changed. It is no longer the party of Mandela, Sisulu, Tambo and Mbeki,' and calling on voters to act on their anger over Nkandla by voting for the DA.[16]

The second campaign video proved even more popular on social media, especially after the SABC refused to air it on the grounds that it incited 'violence against the police officers and attacked Zuma without giving him a right of reply'.[17] In the video, Maimane is in a bathroom washing his face. He looks at himself in the mirror and then starts a 45-second-long monologue on the ANC's failings in power. These range from rising job losses and corruption to police brutality against protestors. '*iANC Ayisafani*' – the ANC is no longer the same, Maimane concludes his monologue.

The Independent Communications Authority of SA, which regulates the country's broadcasting industry, subsequently ruled in favour of the SABC and ordered that the DA remove the part with a photo of a police officer firing rubber bullets at protesting civilians.[18] The DA responded by releasing its 'Ayisafani 2' advert, which, while focusing on the party's growth over the years, also relied on Maimane's talent in front of the camera.

In an article published under his Aloysias Maimane by-line for a Scripture Union magazine in July 2007, Maimane credited the interdenominational Christian youth movement for his involvement in television as well as his other achievements: 'The impact that SU has had in my life has been more far-reaching than the work I did for the organisation. Today I present a Christian TV programme and speak to hundreds of business people each year ... mostly due to the skills and knowledge acquired through SU.'[19]

At the time he wrote this Maimane had already made a name for himself in the church movement; he was gaining a reputation as a talented public speaker at business functions and had become a consultant on diversity in the workplace.

Speakersinc.co.za, one of the agencies that marketed him for public speaking gigs at the time, described Aloysias Maimane as a young talent whose upbringing in Soweto together with his 'excellent education at various institutions' provided him with 'the background to be able to transcend racial barriers'.[20] Another agency called him a 'keynote presenter and facilitator' with 'a particular passion for understanding diversity and for helping companies connect with their top young black talent'.[21]

There is not much information in the public domain relating to the kind of counsel Aloysias Maimane gave to his clients about diversity in the workplace, or as to how they could retain black talent. But a couple of blogs he posted on the TomorrowToday website in 2006 and 2007 give us a glimpse of what he thought of such concepts as ubuntu, affirmative action and youth development before he ventured into active politics.

TomorrowToday is a leadership development group Maimane worked closely with as an associate.[22] Some of the articles are cringeworthy, reflecting the views of a young man who was still struggling to make sense of his world. For instance, in one of them he makes the extraordinary, and obviously false, claim that 'unlike any other people', what best defines Africans is that 'they know how to celebrate'[23] – as if people in other parts of the world do not engage in much celebration of their own.

Continuing in this vein, he further argues that to be welcoming to their African employees, employers must 'create events that help them' celebrate key moments of success at home and in their personal lives. Singing and music, he seems to suggest, should be integral parts of the work environment if it is to be welcoming to these staff members. 'The recent ANC conference,' he said of the ruling party's national policy indaba held in Midrand earlier that month, 'was deemed successful not only because of its content, but also the community and celebration that is created in the passages and corridors of the conference ... Think of the unions: every strike or mass action is associated with song. It is part of the soul of Africa.'[24]

The article even justifies government's penchant for splurging on festivities: 'So, if we have an African government, we will indeed have celebrations. The celebrations will always be big – purely because we can. The criticism is made constantly about how government spends money on celebrations that could be used for other perceived priorities and yet one needs to understand that celebrations speak to the souls of Africans. It is a sociological declaration of success and building of community. It is a requirement.'

This view is in sharp contrast to that firmly held by the DA leader today about government extravagance. For instance, during a party rally in Bethlehem, Free State, late in 2015, Maimane told his supporters that he would 'never come here for Macufe' as the nine-day government-sponsored cultural festival was a waste of taxpayers' money.[25]

Other articles however are more thoughtful. Advising employers on how they can retain their supposedly sought-after and scarce young black talent, the then 26-year-old Maimane tackles some of the reasons behind the 'job hopping' this cohort of employees is often accused of. Young black professionals who change jobs frequently, he argues, do not do so because they are just driven by love of money. Most of them have to support their younger siblings and other members of their extended families and leave their positions for greener pastures in order to make ends meet. 'If you are to successfully hold on to these workers,' he recommends, 'decide what creative types of perks can be given. Look, for example, at innovative ways to incorporate that worker's family into their salary package. A company that would concern itself with the funeral of a family member by making a contribution of some sorts ... would reap warmth and longevity as rewards.'[26]

In another article, whose focus is on managing 'Buppies' – the black and young upwardly mobile professionals – Maimane attempts to make sense of a very thorny issue for post-apartheid young black professionals in the work place: identity. At the workplace, the pre-politician Maimane argues, this generation has 'something of an identity crisis'. He explains: 'It does seem for a black South African to be successful he/she needs to be Western. As in many parts of Africa: West is Best. This means acting and talking (and even dressing) in a western way. This has incredible impact on the way one conducts day to day business.'[27]

Companies can help their employees handle this 'identity crisis' by striving to be more African in their own management styles, he states. This would include adopting leadership approaches which put greater emphasis 'on the community rather than the individual'. 'The paradox is real and evident between a mindset required to succeed in the work world and the "soul" required to remain connected to their community and ancestry. One must not underestimate the power of the pull of the two worlds on today's young black people. Not all of them have been able to fully integrate and reconcile these competing forces.'[28]

If we are to take Speakersinc.co.za's website description of Maimane as someone with 'the background to be able to transcend racial barriers', we would be justified in believing that he was not among those who were not able 'to fully integrate and reconcile these competing forces'. But that does not mean that he always found it easy to 'commute' between the black and the white in his younger days.[29] As we have seen in previous chapters, his exposure to the cross-cultural experience happened very early in life, unusual for a boy growing up in 1980s Soweto, where apartheid, although rapidly dying, still very much regulated who you interacted with on a regular basis.

The invitation to join a Scripture Union camp when he was doing Grade 8 not only led him to convert from Catholicism to evangelism, it also marked the beginning of the multi-cultural experience that was later to help him make it, not only in business, but in politics as well. 'In retrospect,' he once wrote of his early involvement with SU, 'I realise this camp resulted in my decision to follow Jesus ... Even to the simplest of lessons, it gave a cross-cultural experience that was very limited in the 1980s which subsequently made white people "okay" in my eyes.'[30]

It was also through SU that Maimane began his involvement with the NGO sector, especially focusing on youth development. He started working as a volunteer for SU West Rand when he was in Grade 12 and ended up being one of the organisation's directors in that region. By the time he entered formal politics, Maimane had demonstrated his leadership potential while at NGOs such as Child in Crisis Foundation, Siyakholwa Development Foundation and the New Africa Foundation. These organisations are mostly focused on youth development and skills training; also on rural development as well as campaigns aimed at reducing the spread of HIV and Aids.

Maimane's associates in the DA say his passion for youth development has translated into his insistence, since being elected party leader, that high unemployment – which is most acute among young people between the ages of 18 and 35 – should be at the centre of the DA's campaigns.

His past involvement in the NGO sector, they believe, gave him direct experience and understanding of the problems caused by poverty and inequality in many of the country's communities – experience that his predecessors in the DA often lacked. But does that make him come across as more authentic than his predecessors to those poor communities when he goes on the campaign trail? His one major challenge on that score is not that his critics see in him 'an actor' who is merely playing his part in a drama series whose script is written elsewhere. What he has to grapple with is the perception that the party he leads is there primarily to serve the interests of business and the rich, and not the lower social classes.

It is a challenge DA MP Makashule Gana is acutely aware of. He says the party needs to change its character 'so that it becomes a party for all South Africans not only in the way it looks but also in the way it thinks. It should be a party where South Africans look at us and say our aspirations can be realised through the DA.'[31]

To achieve that, the DA would have to be a party 'rooted' in poor communities in the same way that the ANC had been during much of the first two decades of non-racial democracy. 'When we say we are angry about a service delivery issue in a particular area, people must see that we are angry,' says Gana. 'We must be rooted in communities. You can't negate a person's experience of you. So let us not dismiss them when they say "you are speaking like someone in Sandton". What we need is to convince South Africans that we speak for all of them.'

With party structures much stronger and visible in townships, especially those located in metropolitan centres, this is not an impossible goal for the DA to attain. For example, in areas such as Randfontein, on the West Rand, grassroots DA activists have been known to take up civic issues such as the establishment of a crèche for poor working parents who have nowhere to leave their children when they go to work as the established pre-schools in the area are too expensive for them.

CHAPTER 4

....

The battle of public perceptions

'So, will you be voting for him and the DA in the next election?' I asked Kgotla Molefe one early Tuesday evening. I was expecting Molefe to be as unequivocal in his answer as he had been with all other responses to questions about his childhood friend and playmate who was now a famous big-shot politician. But he paused, contemplatively, as if in search of the right words to express his feelings.

We were at a filling station on Steve Kgane Street in Dobsonville's Extension 2 and we had been talking for almost an hour about Molefe's memories of Maimane as a child. The roar from the engines of orange Putco buses that drove down the busy road, bringing passengers back from work in Johannesburg city and its surroundings, was punctuated by the insistent hooting from minibus taxis touting for commuters. Down the street from the petrol station a group of young men were playing a practice soccer match on a dusty field, the same dusty field Maimane and Molefe had honed their football skills on as youngsters.

It is a short distance from the house Maimane grew up in on Mmutle Street. The neighbourhood itself is typically Sowetan – working-class families, the majority of them living in four-room 'matchbox' houses with tiny yards and very few recreational centres. A drive around the area on any given weekday reveals a neighbourhood that, just like many other townships across the country, has been ravaged by the high rate of unemployment among the youth. Young and able-bodied women and men roam around the streets when, like their peers elsewhere, they should be at work making a living.

Maimane must have had these 'unemployed and unemployable' young people in mind when, during his acceptance speech at the DA federal congress in Port Elizabeth, he spoke of 'a tragic story of too many young South Africans' for whom 'the hope and promise of 1994 had no meaning'.[1]

Molefe could have easily been one of them had it not been for his training as a plumber. Although he grew up in the same neighbourhood as Maimane, they did not receive the same kind of education. While Maimane did his primary school at the Catholic Church-run St Angela's, Molefe went to the state-owned Thathezakho Lower Primary. When Maimane was taken out of the township to seek better education, Molefe – who is two years older – proceeded to another local school, Nkolweni Higher Primary.

This is not to say that no one who studied in Bantu Education system schools could ever succeed. There are many who are products of that system and have gone on to make a success of their lives. However the poor quality of education in most township schools, which, sadly, has remained a reality two decades after Bantu Education was officially scrapped from the statutes, means that these institutions churn out thousands of the 'unemployable' every year.

When he left school, Molefe struggled to find a regular job. It was only with the advice of his friends, including Maimane, that he eventually decided to eke out a living as a plumber.

Locals, explained Molefe, were utterly shocked when they first heard the news in 2011 that 'Alu' – the preferred nickname for Maimane in the area – had joined the DA and that he would be running as the party's candidate in the race for the Johannesburg mayoral post. The vast majority, he said, regarded the ANC as their political home, despite the high rate of youth unemployment and persistent complaints about the local government's failure to issue large numbers of them with title deeds. The few who did not support the former liberation movement-turned-governing party favoured other 'black organisations' such as the Pan Africanist Congress, the Azanian People's Organisation or relatively new formations such as Bantu Holomisa's United Democratic Movement and the African People's Convention.

But a 'white party' like the DA? That 'really came as a surprise to many of us because we all grew up following the ANC', Molefe said. There was no hostility towards Maimane, he hastened to explain, just shock. Attitudes have since changed, in fact, and even those who regard the DA as a political opponent pride themselves on having 'a local boy' as the leader of the country's second-biggest party.

Maimane's easy-going personality, which meant that he continued to have friendships in the area regardless of political preferences, helped smooth things over. But the real catalyst for change in the neighbourhood's attitude to him was a massive rodent crisis that was putting the health of Dobsonville residents in danger.

Rats are a major problem in many of Gauteng's townships and informal settlements. Media houses in 2014 reported a case of a month-old baby who was rushed to hospital after having three of her fingers and a portion of her nose chewed off by massive rats in Alexandra township, just across the M1 highway from Sandton.[2] In Ekurhuleni, east of Johannesburg, it is common to hear township residents complain of rats the 'size of puppies'.

A 2011 report compiled by the city of Ekurhuleni blamed increased rodent infestation in the townships on 'poor service delivery resulting in poor sanitation, unkempt open spaces, unmaintained drains, illegal dumping and poor hygiene on private properties'.[3] At one stage, in a desperate bid to eliminate the problem, the Ekurhuleni municipality backed a project that saw the use of owls to catch the rats in Thokoza township. The project failed as most of the owls were reportedly killed by locals.[4]

When confronted by the same crisis, residents of Dobsonville's Extension 2 approached their local councillors and the Johannesburg Metropolitan Council for help. When they could not get any joy, they turned to Maimane. Molefe was impressed: 'He did not hesitate. He sent a truck with a group of DA people who came to clean up the area. Many residents joined them in cleaning up. He is an activist like that, thinking of a practical solution to our problem.'

From then on, continued Molefe, residents started taking an interest in Maimane's political career and the DA: 'Lots of people around here decided to follow the DA because of him. He is a very supportive guy who always encourages people to do the best with their lives.' A lot of people in the area, he said, say they would vote for Maimane.

I then asked him: 'So, will you be voting for him?'

After a long silence, Molefe started by giving the standard 'my vote is my secret' response. He then stated that he would really like to see his old friend succeed and run the country some day and that he was really proud when Maimane was elected to succeed Zille as DA leader. I sensed a 'but' coming. He paused again.

'As gents here *ekasi* [in the township] we sometimes discuss this issue of voting,' he resumed talking, 'what if he wins and then they throw him out and replace him with *ungamla* [a white person]? We don't know if he wins the elections for the DA if he'll be the president or if they will then remove him. The issue is trust, what if they want to put a white person in that position now that he has helped them win? We don't trust them. Deep down we don't trust them.'

THE BATTLE OF PUBLIC PERCEPTIONS

Herein lies Maimane's biggest stumbling block to his quest to grow the DA's share of the votes by attracting more black constituencies over to the party. If a childhood friend who has easy and unfettered access to the DA leader can harbour such fears and suspicions about his role, how can we expect Joe Public to just trust him? The reality staring Maimane in the face is that even though the accusation that he is 'a puppet' for 'white interests' may have started as ANC propaganda aimed at the continued delegitimisation of the DA as a political opponent, it is not just ANC cheerleaders who share this view.

• • •

Social media is not the greatest barometer of voter attitudes, especially in a country like ours where access to technology is heavily dependent on one's race, social class and education. But judging by the social media responses from the young and black constituencies Maimane has to attract to grow the party in a future election, his meteoric rise up the DA hierarchy has been met by more than just a dose of scepticism.

Even as he convincingly won the DA leadership race by close to 90 per cent of the votes, claims that he had been 'anointed' by Zille and that he would be a 'token leader' easily manipulated by the party's 'real powers behind the throne' persisted on social media.

This prompted Maimane to accuse his critics of believing that 'black South Africans' were 'automatons' with no ability to think for themselves: 'Just because someone is black does not mean they can be remote-controlled,' he protested.[5]

At that time Maimane was responding to scathing criticism from social-media commentators such as Khaya Dlanga who saw his rapid rise to become the party's 2014 candidate for Gauteng mayor as an attempt to woo disaffected middle-class black voters who did not trust Zille and the party. Dlanga remarked that, as election day approached, there were fewer posters of Zille than those of Maimane's face in Gauteng, making the latter seem like the party leader: 'Unfortunately, many people see Maimane as something of a puppet, that there are powers behind the operation that are not black. So they are suspicious about the agenda of the people behind him. His emergence has been far too sudden for people to trust him.'[6]

Maimane was to encounter the same accusation soon after his election as DA leader a year later in an interview with the BBC's Zeinab Badawi on HARDtalk: 'Are you a puppet and are there white people controlling the levers of power in the DA?' she pointedly asked him.[7]

'It is the most unfortunate legacy of our past that people want to believe that if you are black in another party, you must be somebody's puppet. It is an insult to black people to suggest that we are incapable of thinking, and therefore, incapable of leading,' Maimane responded.

On the day the interview was broadcast, the DA's detractors had a field day on social media celebrating that Maimane had been 'grilled' and 'exposed' for being 'a puppet'. Sports minister Fikile Mbalula led the charge on Twitter: 'I just watched #BBCHardTalk where Maimane 'Obama' was cornered by the presenter and exposed as a man suffering from poverty of politics,' he gloated.

I met Maimane for coffee in Sandton a few days later while his handling of the HARDtalk interview was still a raging debate on social media and newspapers. He was amused by the reaction, wondering aloud if Mbalula and the other critics would have fared better had they been the ones facing tough questions.

HARDtalk has a reputation for being rough for politicians. In the mid-2000s, at the height of President Thabo Mbeki's controversial stance on

THE BATTLE OF PUBLIC PERCEPTIONS

HIV/Aids, the show's producers struggled to find any government or ANC leaders to interview, as none of them wanted to face the then host of the show, Tim Sebastian. The producers had apparently wanted Mbeki, whom he had interviewed in 2001, but the government communications team just would not let that happen. Manto Tshabalala-Msimang, the controversial health minister, was also discouraged by his office from availing herself for the interview. It eventually fell to the always-cool Kgalema Motlanthe (then ANC secretary-general) to face Sebastian's questions. It was not pretty and Motlanthe did not come out of it unscathed.

Maimane believed he tackled the 'puppet' accusation well on BBC and hoped that with time, the electorate would see it as nothing but the ANC's 'pathetic election strategy' of painting the DA as a 'white party' concerned only with 'protecting white interests'. But six months into his new position, he was still fighting off the same accusation, this time fuelled by two racial incidents he could not have imagined would happen under his watch.

The first was sparked by party MP Dianne Kohler Barnard and her re-posting of a controversial Facebook post by her friend Paul Kirk comparing former state president PW Botha favourably to the post-apartheid government. The second incident occurred at the beginning of 2016 when estate agent Penny Sparrow, at the time a card-carrying DA member, wrote on social media calling black revellers at a KwaZulu-Natal beach on New Year's Day 'monkeys'. Both incidents had seriously negative political ramifications for Maimane and the DA. Suddenly Maimane wasn't just fighting claims that he was 'a puppet'; the party he led was now being accused of harbouring hard-core white racists.

Ironically, in both incidents, the DA's KwaZulu-Natal leader, Zwakele Mncwango – who was elected to the post a month before Maimane became the federal leader – played a central role. The soft-spoken electrical engineering graduate became the KZN leader at the end of April 2015 after narrowly defeating the incumbent Sizwe Mchunu in an election. Mchunu and Kohler Barnard were close, and were regarded as belonging to the same camp in a divided KZN DA ahead of the provincial election. There was a lot of bad blood between the two camps.

Late on 15 September of the same year, Mncwango received information that Kohler Barnard had re-posted a Facebook message on her wall that could put the DA in trouble as she was a high-profile politician with a large following. Kirk, a journalist who, like Kohler Barnard, had taken a keen interest in the ongoing battle between KZN head of the Hawks Johan Booysen and his police superiors, had written about the police suspending Booysen from his job again: 'This is a bloody circus,' Kirk commented in his post, 'Please come back PW Botha – you were far more honest than any of these ANC rogues, and you provided a far better service to the public.'

When he learned of this Mncwango was horrified. He tried several times to get hold of Kohler Barnard over the phone without success. At 6:55 am, he sent her an e-mail:

'It has been brought to my attention that you re-tweeted or shared post by Paul on social media. SEE ATTACHED. I really don't think any DA public representative should share post *[sic]* praising Apartheid architect Botha. This post will damage DA's good brand and please remove it, if not yet done so.'

Kohler Barnard shot back with an angry reply: 'Yes your spies were quite right. I didn't read it the whole way through. Such a pity your spy/s didn't have the courage to contact me directly but went running to you instead. It was an error and I have corrected ... or does "someone" want me hauled through a disciplinary and thrown out the party now? Have we really come to this?'

In his reply, Mncwango was conciliatory, telling Kohler Barnard that he did not 'really expect this matter to end off on disciplinary hearing'. He said she was 'human and we all make mistakes' and added that he regarded the matter as 'closed' since she had said it 'was an error and it is now corrected'. But Kohler Barnard was in fighting mode, writing that Mncwango's 'cowardly spies will circulate' her post widely and say 'I'm a racist'. However what angered many in the party in KZN most was a line that they say betrays a lack of respect and recognition for Mncwango as the provincial leader. Kohler Barnard wrote: 'That I should be smacked down by you, telling me I am damaging the DA brand – as I am a DA brand ambassador – is an insult I will never forget.'

The Facebook post did get circulated widely, causing a major storm for Maimane, who promptly referred Kohler Barnard to a disciplinary process and stripped her of her position as the party's shadow police minister. At a disciplinary hearing Kohler Barnard pleaded guilty to bringing the party into disrepute and breaching the DA's social media policy. She was given a sentence that involved a fine and losing some of her party positions as well as attending diversity classes. The recommendations were then sent to the party's Federal Executive for endorsements. The Fedex amended the sentence and decided to terminate her membership.

Kohler Barnard took the issue up on appeal and a full panel of the party's Federal Legal Commission sat in Sandton just before Christmas in 2015 and reviewed her case. After submissions by her legal representative, Advocate Barry Roux, the panel overturned the Fedex's decision and decided that the termination of her membership be suspended for the duration of Parliament's term, which was to end in 2019, provided she did not repeat the offence.[8] She was also slapped with a R20 000 fine, which was to be given to an NGO working in the field of reconciliation, and was ordered to resign from all of her positions except that of being an MP.

Maimane's handling of the issue drew criticism from all quarters. Kohler Barnard's sympathisers within the DA believed that the new leader, fearful of a backlash from the ANC and its supporters, had over-reacted by hauling her to a disciplinary hearing when she had already apologised and removed the post. There was also his handling of the decision by Fedex to terminate her membership. Her sympathisers accused Maimane of sending mixed signals to both sets of groups within the party on what he would have liked. Some believed he wanted her out of the party, while others claimed he thought she had been punished enough. The eventual decision to expel her as a member, they felt, was too harsh; it did not fit the crime and the mitigating factors were ignored by Fedex.

Journalist Jan-Jan Joubert, who spoke to me before the termination decision was overturned, said Maimane appeared to tailor his message during the debacle according to his audience. He alleged that Maimane had told supporters at a predominantly white DA meeting in Potchefstroom that he did 'not think Dianne was racist' – and then went on SABC and said he did not believe that she would have shared the post without reading it. Joubert was also unhappy that Maimane would not say publicly how he had voted during the Fedex meeting where Kohler Barnard's membership was terminated.

At the opposite end of the spectrum were critics who said the plan was always for Kohler Barnard to escape with a slap on the wrist, that she was 'too powerful' for Maimane to force her out of the party. The actions taken, from disciplinary hearing to removing her as police shadow minister to expelling her, were merely to hoodwink black voters into believing that under Maimane the party was taking action. To this grouping, Kohler Barnard's reinstatement merely proved that the party was 'soft' on racists.

Maimane was convinced that the manner in which the whole saga was handled by his party was consistent with its constitution, its commitment to the rule of law and justice. He did not want a kangaroo court, and that is why he had left the decision of how Kohler Barnard was to be punished in the hands of the party's disciplinary processes. When Fedex decided to terminate her membership, he left it to the appeals process to come up with a final decision.

Cape Town mayor Patricia de Lille, who is also a member of Fedex, disputed claims that Maimane pushed for Kohler Barnard's expulsion: 'His own words were "allow the process to continue". He did not interfere with due process and he certainly didn't drive the expulsion,' she explained.[9]

Maimane has disputed that the final punishment meted out was lenient. 'We gave her a harsh sentence … a suspended sentence of termination of membership. There has been harshness in the sentence … This is a fine of R20 000, a fine of a terminated membership. So there is an action that has been taken, without doubt.'[10]

As it happened, the fallout over the decision to reinstate Kohler Barnard's membership, as well as to keep her as an MP, was not major. The appeal result came at the same time as an item of news that had the country reeling: Zuma's shock 9 December decision to fire finance minister Nhlanhla Nene and replace him with an ANC backbencher, David 'Des' van Rooyen.

Maimane leapt onto the scandal, asking National Assembly Speaker Baleka Mbete for a vote of no confidence in Zuma. Public attention was once again shifting to the ruling party's leadership crisis. But if he thought the worst was now behind him, he was gravely mistaken.

The majority of South Africans were still on holiday enjoying the festive season when Sparrow took to social media with her angry, insulting and unabashedly racist message. The country was on the edge as racial tensions rose. Amidst it all, Mncwango took to Facebook to confirm that Sparrow was indeed a DA member. Although the party acted swiftly by almost immediately terminating her membership, the attacks came thick and fast. The DA took a serious pounding on social media with its opponents saying the estate agent was but one of scores of racists still within party ranks.

In a bid to further distance his party from her racist remarks and show the public that his party brooked no racism, Maimane decided to write Sparrow an open letter.[11] It was supposed to be angry and personal, an emphatic rebuttal of her racist views. But the letter ended up being a broad political message about all that the DA considers wrong with the country. As a result, it did not have the sort of impact Maimane had hoped for. It certainly did not change the perceptions of people who saw him as a black politician 'fronting' for a 'white' political party.

Towards the end of 2015, commentators such as Aubrey Matshiqi had started asking tough questions about what they perceived to be the DA's 'identity crisis' under an 'indecisive' leader. 'Would the real Mmusi Maimane please stand up, and ... will the real DA sit down,' he quipped in a column.[12] Then *Business Day* associate editor Sam Mkokeli warned that Maimane's failure to act decisively sent out a salient message that he had 'not fully stamped his authority'[13] on the DA.

Maimane was losing the public perception battle.

Then, nine days after writing the open letter to Sparrow, he made an appearance at the Apartheid Museum in Johannesburg for what his communications team had billed as his 'important speech on race and identity'.

It was not the first time that he had come to the venue – which documents the history of apartheid and the resistance movement to it – to talk about race. He had done so in February 2014 while running for the Gauteng premiership. But he was not the DA's overall leader then and his speech at the time seemed more geared to establishing his credentials as an individual who had suffered under apartheid – and hence had similar life experiences to those of the majority of voters – than to present a new vision for South Africa. What made his second Apartheid Museum speech more important, besides the fact that he was now leader and could therefore set policy, was that it was timely, coming when no other politician had shown leadership to a nation that was being ripped apart by racial differences.

THE BATTLE OF PUBLIC PERCEPTIONS

President Jacob Zuma had initially underplayed public anger over Sparrow, telling eNCA in an interview that 'people have tended to exaggerate the issue of racism'; that 'we defeated racism' and that our society is 'a rainbow nation, it is not racial'.[14] A few days earlier, reacting to Maimane's statement that the country was 'leaderless' on the issue because the President had failed to give direction, Zuma had told the nation that racism was a DA problem: 'It has been DA members who have been racist. Why must he blame me, as the leader of DA? He's been called a monkey, why can't he deal with it? Why is he blaming Zuma? C'mon, please!'[15]

• • •

When Maimane and his team made arrangements for his second Apartheid Museum speech, they knew that he would have to do more than merely draw a line between the party and Sparrow or distance the party from those who still believe life was better under PW Botha's rule.

It was a sunny Tuesday morning and there was not even standing room in the museum's auditorium, where the event was to take place. The vast majority of those in the audience were DA public representatives and party activists, mostly donning the party's blue shirts and T-shirts. Maimane looked solemn in his navy blue suit and white shirt. The customary icebreakers, which usually involve him saying something funny about himself, his party or family members, were missing. The mood in the hall was sombre, as were Maimane's words:

'Apartheid may be history, but the racism that nurtured and sustained it continues to this day. Racism demeans us all, black and white. It opens the wounds of its victims and exposes the ignorance of those who perpetrate it. It robs us of the dignity that so many fought for. And racism divides us. Just look at us. At the very moment we need to be standing together, we are being torn apart.'[16]

He reminded his audience of how South Africa's dream of becoming a 'Rainbow Nation' had begun with so much hope under President Nelson Mandela's leadership in 1994: 'He urged us to look beyond our difference and find our common humanity. And so we did.' But 'when the honeymoon ended', South Africans 'found that we hardly knew one another'. Two decades into democracy, 'it feels as though we are drifting apart' and part of the problem is that black South Africans 'are still made to feel inferior because of the colour of their skin'.

To illustrate how deep this inferiority runs in black communities, he recalled how as children in Dobsonville, every successful black person would be called '*ngamla*' – which is township slang for a white person. 'And I cannot tell you how many times I am told by black South Africans that I have "done well" because I happen to be married to a white woman. Apartheid was so dehumanising that, too often, even today, white people remain the benchmark that we set ourselves.'

To further drive the point home about how poverty remained racialised in a democratic South Africa, Maimane quoted a passage from Soweto-born young novelist Niq Mhlongo's celebrated novel, *After Tears*: 'If you're black and you failed to get rich in the first year of our democracy, when Tata Mandela came to power, you must forget it, my bra. The gravy train has passed you by and, like me, you'll live in poverty until your beard turns grey. The bridge between the stinking rich and the poor has been demolished. That is the harsh reality of our democracy.'[17]

Black and white South Africans, said Maimane, need to talk about how they can work together to end this racialised inequality: 'This conversation is interrupted, however, every time a racist incident hits the headlines and explodes onto social media. Suddenly, we are back to square one. The injury of racial inequality is compounded by the insult of racism. It is like pouring salt in a deep wound.'

While acknowledging that the 'vast majority of white people don't think like Penny Sparrow' and that many are playing their part to 'redress the legacy of the past', Maimane said he knew there were still people 'who talk to each other around the braai as if they were living in the 1970s ... And we all know somebody who is fond of starting a sentence with "I'm not a racist, but..."'

Maimane was talking about race and racism in a manner that had not been heard before from a DA leader: 'Because, for every incident of overt racism, there are thousands of instances of casual, everyday racism: Talking down to people, laughing when people pronounce an English word incorrectly ... believing somebody's accent is a sign of their intelligence.'

Maimane was equally critical of black people who make racist statements and then hide behind the claim that black people are not capable of prejudice: 'We all have the capacity for greatness, and we all have the capacity for prejudice,' he said. Quoting from English poet Roger McGough's 'You and I', he appealed to South Africans to stop shouting past each other and, instead, 'find each other again'.

For his part, he was going to start the conversation within his party. He announced a series of dialogues on race called 'Stand Up, Speak Out' and said these would 'involve South Africans from all walks of life'. The dialogues, he promised, would not be conducted under the DA's banner, nor would they be driven by public representatives. As DA leader he realised that it fell upon his shoulders to give direction as to how the party would deal with its own internal racial challenges. Attempting to 'bring people together across the colour line on the basis of shared values,' he said, did not mean that the DA must ignore race. 'Racial injustice is real and we need to redress it. We cannot wish it away by pretending to be colour-blind.' The statement differed sharply from the previous DA rhetoric of 'there are no pink, black, white or green people in the DA; only blue ones'.

Maimane also broke with the old DA approach of either denying racial tensions within its ranks or downplaying them. The DA, he told the audience – which included over a million more people who were watching the proceedings live on their television sets – was 'not perfect'. To fight racism within its ranks, he ordered that members were now to be expected 'not to turn a blind eye to racism no matter how subtle or coded ... Because racists are not welcome in the DA. And if you're a racist and you are thinking of voting for the DA, please don't. We are not the party for you.'

Brave words, especially for a new leader, one who has not fully won the confidence of some of the more conservative constituencies that drifted towards the DA with the collapse of the New National Party over a decade ago. It was by winning over these constituencies that Tony Leon grew the DA to the position where it became the country's official opposition party. Zille increased the support base further by striking a balance between winning new constituencies while keeping the ones already within the fold loyal.

Was Maimane at risk of chasing away the DA's more conservative white voters with his rhetoric?

In October 2015 I asked Ian Ollis if Maimane's drive to win over large chunks of black urban voters away from the ANC would not end up alienating some of the party's traditional white voters. He disagreed: 'Let me tell you, the voters in Sandton are in my constituency and they are enthusiastic about Mmusi. I had a constituency meeting on Monday night and we had 45 people; about 30 of them want to be DA councillors and serve under Mmusi Maimane. So I don't see people leaving. You might find one racist or two who might vote for someone else. But you must remember South Africans realise that you can't vote for the smaller parties as it is a waste of time.

So you might find one or two racist white people who won't vote because Mmusi Maimane is black, but they are a small number.'[18]

To show that he was serious about not tolerating racism in the party he leads, Maimane introduced an 'anti-racism pledge' that will have to be signed by every new or returning member when they join the DA. It reads:

> I pledge to uphold the values of the Constitution, to cherish its vision for a united, non-racial, democratic South Africa, and to nourish this vision in my personal conduct.
>
> I acknowledge that Apartheid was an evil system, and recognise that its legacy remains reflected in the unequal structure of South African society today.
>
> I reject discrimination in all its forms, and pledge to help root it out wherever I encounter it in South Africa.
>
> I will not perpetuate racial division, and will never undermine the dignity of my fellow South Africans.
>
> Instead, I will commit myself to working to overcome inequality and achieving shared prosperity.[19]
>
> Any member found to be in violation of the pledge will be expelled.

More controversially, Maimane then announced that the DA will set targets for the recruitment and development of candidates who will make the party more 'diverse' in the National Assembly and other legislatures. He did not call them quotas, but it was clear what he wanted: 'My objective is to ensure that, by 2019, our parliamentary and legislature caucuses, and our decision-making structures at all levels, reflect the diversity of our complex society.'

It is a bold vision, one which Maimane would not have even imagined if he was 'the puppet' his detractors try to paint him as. When I spoke to Ollis in 2015, he suggested that the party had already embarked along this path, pointing out that seven out of the nine party provincial leaders were already black: 'What the public has not realised is that right now, only two provincial leaders are white. There is this focus on Maimane, but what about the others?'

Seen from that perspective the party has made great strides. But looking at the DA from various other angles, Maimane has his work cut out. About two thirds of the party's 89 parliamentarians are white. If it is to be 'more representative' by the 2019 elections, a lot of its current MPs will not be returning, which could be a source of instability and uncertainty for the party. According to the *Sunday Times*, at the beginning of 2016, the DA's senior staff complement of 31 people is 68 per cent white and its seven-member senior executive team has six whites and one South African of Indian heritage.[20]

Writing in her *Business Day* column a few days after Maimane's groundbreaking speech, former DA parliamentary leader Lindiwe Mazibuko described it as an 'outstanding initiative'. She cautioned, however, that Maimane's 'Stand Up, Speak Out' initiative will be meaningless if it does not happen within the party as well: 'The party should reflect, among other things, on a culture that isolates black members and leaders, calling them a "black caucus" and branding them "illiberal racial nationalists" if they openly socialise with one another, and discouraging them from forming bonds of friendship and familiarity.'[21]

In other words, the whole culture, not just the numbers, would have to change to make the party more representative and attractive to more South Africans.

Mazibuko also revealed the existence of a 'hurtful and inaccurate internal party narrative' that presumes 'white competence' and labels 'black leaders products of the generosity of white counterparts'. These are damning claims, especially coming from a former senior party leader – one who was once seen as Zille's heir apparent.

However, if Maimane is to succeed in turning the DA into an inclusive party that is attractive to both black and white voters, he will have to follow his moving speeches up with decisive action. At the time of writing, three months after the announcement of the 'Stand Up, Speak Out' initiative, there had been no activity associated with it announced.

Without the changes he promised taking off the ground, potential voters like his childhood friend Kgotla Molefe will continue to wonder if indeed he is now the guy in charge at the DA. He will continue having to field the question wherever he goes: Are you a puppet?

CHAPTER 5

Dirty tricks in Bethlehem

October 2015, Eastern Free State: Maimane and his entourage were door-to-door campaigning in Bohlokong township when news came that the hall booked for the DA mass rally later that morning was locked and that the caretaker had disappeared with the keys. Rally organisers were furious, seeing the caretaker's vanishing act as nothing but a ploy by the ANC-controlled Dihlabeng Local Municipality (which owns and runs the community hall in question) to sabotage their gathering. Local government elections were still almost a year away and already the DA's opponents were playing dirty, and in Bethlehem of all places.

This nondescript rural town, noticeable only for its biblical name and known only for its Voortrekker High School which educated – among others – the country's second-last apartheid president, PW Botha, could not by any stretch of the imagination be described as a closely contested area for the ANC and the DA.

So why the dirty tricks?

Maimane was in Bohlokong, a tiny township outside of Bethlehem, as part of his two-day visit to the province to promote the DA's Vision 2029.

With a total population of just over 50 000, the impoverished township is the archetype of economically struggling former blacks-only labour reserves dotting Free State's farming towns. Unemployment rates are extremely high and the delivery of basic services such as water, sanitation and decent public health services is poor. Yet the governing ANC continues to enjoy overwhelming support.

In the 2011 local government elections, the ruling party won 30 of the 40 available council seats. The DA only managed eight, while Cope and the Freedom Front Plus got one seat each. Since those elections, a number of ANC activists in the area have broken away and joined the EFF, but Malema's party in Bethlehem, as in most of the Free State, has struggled to make any serious inroads into traditional ANC strongholds.

Yet in the days leading up to Maimane's visit to the area, one would have been forgiven for believing that Bohlokong, Bethlehem and the rest of the Dihlabeng municipality's continued rule by the ANC was in serious jeopardy. A pamphlet was apparently distributed in the area calling on locals to 'defend the ANC' by not attending the DA rally. According to Maimane, a nearby venue that was initially earmarked for the gathering was suddenly made unavailable by authorities.[1] This was despite the fact that the party had paid a R400 deposit for that hall.

The DA then opted for Bohlokong New Community Hall, where organisers were told to pay R5 000 to secure the use of the venue. They duly paid the amount. But when the organisers went to the hall on Friday night to prepare the venue for the Sunday rally, they were refused permission to enter the premises. They were told that they could not because the venue was scheduled to host 'yet another event' the very next day.[2] Two days later, the caretaker had gone missing, with the keys to the venue also nowhere to be found. The municipality blamed it all on its 'cleaning staff' which, it said, had cleaned the hall after a Saturday function and then 'left the bundle of keys of the hall complex in the supervisor's office but forgot to make the supervisor aware'.[3] The caretaker then 'unknowingly' locked the keys to the hall inside his office and left town. By the time it was discovered that the keys were in his office, the 'supervisor was hundreds of kilometres away from Bethlehem attending to important family matters', concluded the municipality.

DA supporters, many of whom arrived in buses and minibus taxis, were swelling with anger as they found the venue under lock and key. Some of them started threatening to break down the doors and force their way in. But before the situation got out of hand, DA leaders – who were also as agitated as their members – summoned the services of a local locksmith. Later on, after they had gained access, a defiant DA Free State leader Patricia Kopane told supporters that the saga was an act of desperation on the part of the ANC and the municipality. She defended the decision to hire a locksmith and force open the doors to the hall 'because it belonged to the people, not to the ANC'.[4]

When I spoke to Maimane later that morning, he intimated that such 'acts of intimidation and abuse of power' by the ANC were becoming common. To him this indicated that 'the DA's growth' was threatening the ANC's dominance. Just the previous day during his visit to the provincial capital, Mangaung, he added, the DA had been prevented from holding a meeting at a local public park.

If the intention of the lockout was to rattle the new DA leader a bit, the tactics seemed to have failed by the time he took to the stage to address the several hundreds of enthusiastic party faithful gathered in the hall to listen to him. If anything, Maimane seemed to be in an uncharacteristically defiant mood that morning, calling on supporters not to be meek in the face of intimidation by opponents: 'We will show them we are a new DA that is brave, that has no fear,' he said, 'This is no time to sleep, people must see you in the taxis ... I encourage you to wear your blue T-shirts everywhere.'[5]

The rally at times resembled an evangelical church service as Maimane and other party leaders sporadically broke into song in the middle of speeches. Some gave testimony-like speeches on why they had chosen 'the blue wave' while others – apparently former EFF members – were paraded to the audience as new converts, complete with brand new blue T-shirts.

Chants of '*Obama warona, Obama oteng!* Our Obama, Obama is here!' reverberated through the hall as Maimane was introduced by the Masters of Ceremony to the crowd as 'the next president of South Africa'. '*Zuma wa tseba, Malema wa tseba, iyeza ibhoza* (Zuma knows, Malema knows, the real McCoy is coming)', the crowd sang in a mixture of seSotho and isiZulu.

Maimane had come to Bohlokong well aware that if the DA is to continue on its growth trajectory and become a future government, he will have to box cleverly by devoting his energies to attacking the ANC's soft underbelly. In the Bethlehem area that soft underbelly was the Dihlabeng Regional Hospital, a public health facility that had been in the news for all the wrong reasons.

A special *Mail & Guardian* investigation into the state of public hospitals in the province uncovered shocking evidence of negligence as well as failure to fill key positions and order medical equipment and stock. Doctors at the hospital who spoke to the newspaper on condition of anonymity said they were even considering resigning because of terrible working conditions there: 'We can't tell patients the real reasons why we can't help them. We can't tell them there's a lack of staff and medication and no will from the provincial health department to fix it. We are obliged to be loyal to our employer. We just tell patients "we unfortunately can't do anything more for you,"' one of the doctors told the newspaper.[6]

In his speech to Bohlokong party supporters, Maimane put the blame squarely at the door of Free State premier Ace Magashule (who is also provincial ANC chairman) and Health MEC Benny Malakoane: 'Dihlabeng Hospital is still a painful reminder of everything that is wrong with the Free State government ... And it is not alone. Across the length and breadth of the province, state hospitals are crumbling, their shelves stand empty, their patients sleep on the floor and their doctor and nursing positions remain vacant.'

The Magashule government, he added, had no money to hire new doctors and buy new linen and medical supplies for Dihlabeng – and yet saw nothing wrong with paying R140 million for a government website redesign.[7] It did not surprise him that Magashule and others in the ANC were misbehaving, Maimane continued, because the rot had started at the top with President Zuma: 'If Zuma does Nkandla corruption, how can he expect the likes of Ace to behave?'

But even as he went for the jugular, Maimane seemed pretty well aware of his own party's soft underbelly, which had been exposed in a dramatic fashion a few days earlier. The Free State leg of Vision 2029 came at the end of what the *Sunday Times* had, that morning, dubbed as Maimane's 'most embarrassing week' as DA leader.[8]

It all began on Wednesday, 30 September, when the DA lost a ward it should have won easily during a by-election in the Theewaterskloof Municipality, which includes Caledon, in the Western Cape. A day later, Maimane suffered a heavy blow as the Kohler Barnard Facebook scandal broke. Now battling to put out a number of fires, the DA was slapped with another controversy as the Supreme Court of Appeal dismissed a bid by the Thembu monarch, King Buyelekhaya Dalindyebo, to have his convictions on a number of serious crimes overturned.

When the king joined the DA ahead of the 2014 general election, Maimane, Zille and Eastern Cape party leader Athol Trollip had proudly paraded him as a big catch who would help the DA gain rural voters in the former Transkei. They did this even though they knew that the controversial monarch's criminal case was still on appeal. Now that he had lost his appeal and was about to begin his prison sentence, critics were questioning the DA's wisdom in associating itself with such a compromised and polarising individual. The king was simply not worth the trouble he was causing the DA, especially considering that his membership had brought the party no significant gains in Thembuland during the 2014 elections.

Although Maimane publicly defended the DA's decision to recruit Dalindyebo,[9] he was more than pleased to see the back of him: the king's membership was terminated a day after the Supreme Court ruling: 'The king was easy,' stated an associate. 'That was a [DA] constitutional issue; all it took was a phone call to say terminate his membership.'

But what proved most difficult for Maimane as the weekend unfolded was the Kohler Barnard matter. Though he had acted immediately after the news broke, this did not satisfy his critics at both ends of the political spectrum. Kohler Barnard's sympathisers accused him of playing to the gallery at the expense of one of the party's hardest working and most prominent parliamentarians. On the other hand, a DA leader sympathetic to Maimane likened his decision to haul her through a disciplinary process to Thabo Mbeki's 2005 decision to fire Zuma as the country's deputy president following the Schabir Shaik corruption trial. Like Mbeki, he was 'taking on one of the senior members of the party' who also happened to be popular with a particular section of the organisation. 'But that is the job of leadership, you have to take some tough decisions at times. He had to send a strong message to the party to say "stop this nonsense".'

However not everyone was convinced that the steps taken against Kohler Barnard had been strong enough. Maimane's critics on the left, especially ANC-leaning commentators on social media platforms such as Twitter and Facebook, were having a field day using the debacle as 'evidence' that the DA applied race-based double standards when it came to taking action against errant members. Why was King Dalindyebo summarily expelled and Kohler

Barnard taken through a disciplinary process, demanded 'Black Twitter', a community of black commentators.

At a post-rally press conference in Bohlokong, Maimane provided the answer: 'We took two decisions ... We removed Dalindyebo's membership immediately, we didn't ask questions because that is consistent with our constitution. When it comes to Ms Kohler Barnard, we initiated a disciplinary hearing, let the party deal with it.'[10] He was frustrated by the continued comparison of the two cases: 'This is the thing that people don't understand. They think that if you are a leader you wake up and phone and say "hey you used to be with us but now you no longer work for us". That is what happens in other parties that are run by dictators. In our party we have institutions that investigate things and deal with them.'

But it was not just 'Black Twitter' that was demanding a hard-line approach. According to his close associates, Maimane was inundated that week with calls from grassroots party activists who complained that the Kohler Barnard debacle was making it difficult for them to campaign in the townships and other predominantly black areas. 'On the ground activists face a difficult challenge,' said one. 'When they arrive at someone's house and then they get told "but you want to look back to apartheid"... These are people who would normally give us a chance to speak to them as they feel corruption and are looking for an alternative. That is why Mmusi has to act, he does not only lead MPs and MPLs, he also leads the guy on the street who works day to day for us. That guy too has to be heard.'

In an attempt to assuage this constituency, which demanded swift action out of both anger and fear that the issue would be used to paint the DA racist, Maimane that weekend announced drastic changes to his 'shadow cabinet' in Parliament.[11] The greatest beneficiaries of this reshuffle were black MPs such as Phumzile van Damme, who took over the communications portfolio, Zakhele Mbhele, who replaced the demoted Kohler Barnard in the police portfolio, and Thomas Hadebe, who was given environmental affairs. But even that could not satisfy Maimane's critics, many of them seeing the reshuffle move as a PR stunt.

Among the most vocal sceptics, for obvious reasons, was ANC parliamentary spokesman Moloto Mothapo. An active participant on Twitter, Mothapo made a meal out of the fact that it was Zille, not Maimane, who first publicly demanded that Kohler Barnard remove the offensive post from her Facebook page. 'Interesting, Zille first to order Kohler-Barnard to apologise (7:23). Mmusi followed 1hr later (8:39). Who call shots?'[12] Zille had tweeted: '@DKB20 Please withdraw that post and apologise unconditionally. It is indefensible, even if you missed the PW Botha bit.'[13] Maimane had later written: 'The post by @DKB20 is indefensible. She has withdrawn it and apologised now our internal disciplinary processes will be dealing with this.'[14]

When the storm over the Facebook post first broke on Twitter, Maimane was in the air on his way to the Eastern Cape for a meeting with students at the University of Fort Hare's Alice campus. This however did not stop his political opponents from claiming that he was taking instructions from his predecessor and that, had Zille not spoken out, Maimane would not have had the courage to call Kohler Barnard out.

This irritated Maimane: 'Helen Zille tweets once, now suddenly they say "you see Helen Zille is running the organisation". How fearful must you be? How inferior must you feel that a person tweets once and now suddenly she runs the organisation? It is nonsense!'[15]

• • •

Accompanying Maimane on this Free State leg of his Vision 2029 nationwide tour were his wife Natalie and their daughter, Kgalaletso. Given how difficult the week had proved to be for him, it was no surprise that he had turned to his family unit for support. By all accounts, they are a close-knit family: in a video interview with Netwerk24 soon after Maimane's election as DA leader, Natalie described her husband as her 'best friend'.

The two were both already devout Christians when they met through church circles in 1999. Over time their friendship grew into a full-blown romance: 'It wasn't a whirlwind romance,' Natalie told Netwerk24, 'he was like my best friend. Plus he is hot.' As the relationship grew, Maimane once said, their attraction became increasingly 'based on common values'. 'To say I did not see she was white and she did not see I was black would be disingenuous, but we were able to look past this.'[16] But that didn't mean the outside world would do the same and let the two young lovebirds be.

Barely a decade after the end of official apartheid, and less than 20 years since the scrapping of the Prohibition of Mixed Marriages Act and the Immorality Act, loving across the colour line was still regarded as taboo by some. The two pieces of legislation made it illegal to have a romantic relationship with a person of a different racial group. Even though the laws were repealed by PW Botha's government in 1985 as part of his desperate attempt to placate foreign governments and companies who were demanding an end to apartheid, their effects remained on many people's psyches.

Sowetan columnist Mapula Nkosi once confessed in her column that when she saw 'a black and white couple walking down the street … my eyes followed them until they turned the corner'.[17] She just did not see the relationship for what it was, immediately concluding that the white male in his fifties was rich and that the black woman she presumed to be much younger was in it for reasons other than romance. 'I was so intent on finding some dirty or weird reasons to explain something as natural and as simple as attraction and love,' Nkosi wrote.

Mmusi and Natalie were confronted by similar reactions when they went out in public in those early days of their romance. 'It took time to accept stereotypical responses. For example, we would go to a mall and another black South African would applaud me, as though I'd achieved something extraordinary, and some white South Africans would look down on us as if it were an unnatural occurrence. But mostly, it was important for us to be with each other – not fight a cause, not prove a point, but simply be.'[18]

According to Maimane, these 'historical factors' also came into play when he took Natalie to meet his family for the first time one evening.[19] Both of them were nervous, albeit for different reasons. Natalie was the first girlfriend he was taking to meet his parents at home in Dobsonville.

'Natalie was nervous because I had explained to her that she would be treated differently because she is white, that she would have to work harder than other girls to gain my parents' trust.' And so they devised a plan: 'We agreed that on the first meeting my wife would not accept tea, she would instead make tea in the home of my parents. With that gesture, she showed that she did not have a superiority complex, that she was willing to make a gesture, however small, to gain acceptance.'[20]

For a mixed-race South African couple, Mmusi and Natalie are refreshingly open about their racial differences and the realities associated with them. Often couples in similar relationships say they 'don't see colour', but Maimane often says 'if you don't see that I am black then you don't see me'. As he puts it, 'On the outside we are different from each other, even our children are different from us. We are a South African family. My wife and I would just have to adopt an Indian child and we could be the Rainbow Nation. But remove race from the equation, and we're not very different.'[21]

Natalie told Netwerk24 that non-racialism is 'not about not seeing colour. It is about seeing one another and understand the history each person comes from and making space for that person and finding commonality in that space. But you can't ignore that part of a person's identity ...'

The couple married in 2005 after what Natalie described to one journalist as a 'quite elaborate' New Year's Eve that involved several of their friends.[22] It all began with a dinner at an upmarket hotel which was followed by him blindfolding and driving her to Walter Sisulu Botanical Gardens, in western Johannesburg. According to Natalie, Mmusi had arranged that the Botanical Gardens be opened just for them. He had set up a picnic where they could watch the waterfall tumble down and could hear its melody as it poured over rocks: 'A whole lot of lanterns lit up all the way and roses ... and he played our song [Nat King Cole's 'When I fall in love'], and he asked me to marry him.'[23]

In true South African township fashion, their elaborate wedding was done over two legs. Their church hosted the white wedding and a traditional 'African wedding' was held at the Maimane home in Dobsonville. Natalie – who hails from Florida in Roodepoort, not too far from Dobsonville – is now an integral part of the Maimane clan in the township. According to Mmusi's childhood friend Kgotla, who still resides in the township, it is not uncommon to see Natalie driving into the neighbourhood on her own, visiting her husband's family.

Maimane tells an interesting story to illustrate the road they, as a family, have travelled to transcend the racial barriers they feared on that first day he took Natalie to meet his parents. They had returned from burying one of their relatives when Natalie and 'another cousin of ours who is married into the family' joined a queue of those waiting for food. My grandmother came across and literally gave them a tongue lashing, saying 'you are standing in the line when everybody is working'.[24]

Maimane says the incident demonstrated to him that his family had fully accepted Natalie as one of their own. 'They just thought "you are a woman in our house, get your act together and serve". When I remember that story, it kind of reminds me of the journey that we have been on.'[25]

At home, the Maimanes try to raise their children in a manner that will lead them to fully embrace their identities. When their eldest child, daughter Kgalaletso, was born Natalie gave her the name because she wanted her to have a seTswana first name. Maimane has said in various interviews that they try to raise Kgalaletso and her brother Kgosi as speakers of both English and seTswana. Like most other young and black middle-class parents who raise their children in the formerly white suburbs, Maimane's greatest frustration – having grown up in a bilingual family with a mother who taught them isiXhosa while their father spoke to them mostly in seTswana – is that there aren't enough 'reinforcers', such as seTswana nursery rhymes and fairy tales, available to children at their schools.

But if the couple's extended family and their community at large treat their multi-racial relationship as 'normal', it has not always been the same in the world of politics. 'When Mmusi started working in Parliament,' complained Natalie, 'the idea that he was married to a white woman was brought up ... several times by MPs who heckled him ... Sadly, it gets brought up by the ANC as sort of a hole in his Africanness, that because he is married to a white woman, he is not African enough.'[26]

Of course, Maimane was not the first prominent South African political figure to be involved in a multi-racial relationship. Since the dawn of freedom there have been a number of mixed couples that no one frowned upon or used to suggest that, by marrying across the racial line, a politician had somehow 'betrayed' his race. Instead couples such as former Gauteng premier and human settlements minister Tokyo Sexwale and his second wife Judy were celebrated as symbols of Nelson Mandela's Rainbow Nation and shining examples of how apartheid had finally been defeated.

Maimane's labelling by his rival MPs as being 'not black enough' simply because he is married to a white woman should not be seen in isolation from the general attack strategy the ANC – and to some extent the EFF – has adopted towards black DA MPs. In his past life as ANC Youth League president, Julius Malema used to call the DA's Lindiwe Mazibuko Zille's 'tea girl'. Higher education minister and SA Communist Party leader Blade Nzimande, during a 2011 parliamentary debate, called Mazibuko 'a coconut' because of her 'Model-C English' accent.

When Maimane replaced Mazibuko as DA parliamentary leader in 2014, it took no time before ANC MPs, such as sports minister Fikile Mbalula, started calling him a 'token black' who was in the position merely to serve his white masters. By these accusations, the ANC hopes to delegitimise black DA MPs in the eyes of voters as inauthentic leaders and hired hands who are only there to advance the interests of 'former oppressors'. Black politicians in predominantly – and historically – white parties should not be trusted by the previously oppressed, the message from the ruling party seems to be.

For Maimane, such slurs are an indication of just how far the ruling party has drifted from the non-racialism ideals of Mandela and other leaders of the liberation struggle: 'When people stand up in Parliament saying things like "Maimane is only a token black who was hired because he is married to a white person", almost attacking in really racial language, nobody says a thing,' he observed.[27]

However, it emerged in the weeks running up to the DA Port Elizabeth federal congress that elected Maimane as Zille's successor that ANC MPs were not the only ones labelling Maimane 'not black enough' because of his marriage to Natalie. A rumour started doing the rounds in Gauteng media circles in late April of that year that some members of the DA 'black caucus' were not keen on Maimane because – among other things – they believed that his marriage to a white woman would put off some black voters.

The rumours remained just that among journalists until, later that year – six months after Maimane had taken over the party leadership – a three-page letter on the official party letterhead and signed off by DA federal chairman

Athol Trollip emerged.[28] It was addressed to the Western Cape deputy leader, an MEC in Zille's provincial cabinet, Bonginkosi Madikizela. In the letter Trollip confronted Madikizela on claims that the latter had told some delegates during the federal congress that Maimane was 'not good enough because he is married to a white woman' and that black members of the party should not 'allow a situation where Mmusi become [sic] the only black leader'.

Trollip said he initially 'could hardly believe my ears' when he was told of Madikizela's alleged statements and that he was 'shattered when I was shown an SMS conversation confirming this … Not only are these utterances deeply racist, they are offensive to everyone involved, and by involved I mean Mmusi's wife, Natalie and all the candidates who stood for various positions.' He also expressed concern over what he termed as emergence of racial nationalism within the DA in the run-up to the federal congress.

The *Sunday Times* reported that both Trollip and Madikizela had confirmed the letter, with the latter, who denies ever uttering such words about Maimane and his wife, saying they eventually resolved the matter. 'These were just false rumours. There were no e-mails or Whatsapps like that,' he said.[29]

The saga gives us just a snippet of the behind-the-scenes tensions that engulfed the DA during the gruelling campaign for the job of Zille's successor.

Through it all, the Maimanes seemed to be taking it in their stride. When an anonymous e-mail alleging a sex scandal within the DA was circulated just days before the federal congress, Natalie took to Twitter to defend her partner: '16 years of friendship, 10 years of marriage. I know of @MmusiMaimane. He's the real deal. The mud will simply wash off,' she tweeted.

A few days after Maimane won, Natalie told journalist Bianca Capazorio that as campaigns go, the race 'was probably one of the easier ones and I think it wasn't as bad as what it looked because it was something I'd become used to'. Mmusi had told her about the e-mail days before it surfaced in public and she had believed that he was the victim of a smear campaign. 'Because

I know my husband, the characteristics used to describe him are just so far from who he is that I could just look at it and go: "It's not true", she said.[30]

To support her husband's political ambition, Natalie decided to be a stay-at-home mom, leaving behind her career teaching history and English. As we have seen in a previous chapter, she was instrumental in Maimane's decision to enter politics, first convincing him that the spiritual message he had received about a young man who had neglected his calling to politics was for him. When he finally accepted this, she supported his decision to return to university and further his studies in preparation of a new career. Even Maimane's political rivals acknowledge the role she has played in his political career, although they tend to cast it in a negative light.

• • •

Ahead of the 2014 general election, the ANC in Gauteng had been seriously worried about how it was going to perform at the polls. Public anger over e-tolls as well as President Jacob Zuma's unpopularity in the province, the ANC feared, would cost the party support at the polls, especially among middle-class voters who constituted 25 per cent of those registered to vote.

The political landscape had also changed with the formation of the EFF – which was expected to attract youth voters away from the ANC – and the introduction of Maimane as the DA's premier candidate.

To keep the black middle class from seeing the DA as a viable alternative, some of the ANC leaders in the province had started putting out feelers to see if they could entice Maimane to the ANC. It would have been a great scoop for the party, one that would have completely collapsed the DA's R100-million election campaign in the province.

But when it became clear that Maimane's star was rapidly rising within the DA, with indications already that an even greater role awaited him at national level after the elections, his would-be recruiters had blamed Natalie for his lack of interest. One of the Gauteng ANC personalities, said to have had knowledge of the intimate details of a plan to win Maimane over, had told *Sunday Times* journalist Sibongakonke Shoba that Natalie had 'too much influence' over her husband and that this was the main reason Maimane had turned them down. When Shoba asked Maimane about the ANC's approach at the time, he neither confirmed nor denied it.

Maimane would not have been the only black DA leader in the ANC's sights ahead of the elections. Several others – some of them in KwaZulu-Natal – were recruited in what was clearly an attempt by the ruling party to destabilise its competitor's election campaign.

With or without Natalie's help, Maimane would have seen through the ruling party's intentions and would have known that he would be better off staying put in the DA. But there is no denying that he involves her in all the major decisions relating to his career. It was therefore no surprise that she was by his side in Bohlokong, Bethlehem, during a week in which his leadership mettle was tested for the first time since he took over from Zille.

CHAPTER 6

....

'Where we govern, we govern better'

MAIMANE MAY NEVER BE ABLE TO convince all of his detractors that he is no puppet. Even if he were to successfully implement all the changes he promised at the Apartheid Museum and transform all party structures to make them reflect the country's demographics, there would always be those who saw in him 'a rented black' – and in the DA, a 'white party'.

Given South Africa's past, it is no surprise that identity politics remains a profitable political enterprise. Racial mobilisation has characterised the political party system since the formation of the Union of South Africa in 1910. The collapse of the apartheid system did not put an end to this: support for political parties at the polls has continued to be along racial lines. Even with the universally celebrated Nelson Mandela at the helm, the ANC struggled to win votes among the country's minorities, while parties such as the National Party and the Democratic Party got their votes mainly from those constituencies.

Tony Leon grew the Democratic Party, and subsequently the DA, by consolidating the party's support among minorities. Helen Zille used this strong base, and the DA's status as the official opposition, to try and convince black voters that her party was the only viable alternative to the ANC. Maimane will be judged not only on whether he succeeds in 'transforming' the DA, but on whether he is able to increase its share of the votes to the point where it poses a real threat to the ruling party.

The DA has been growing with every election since 1994, at which its predecessor, the DP, won just 1.7 per cent of the votes. The percentage had grown to 12.4 by the 2004 elections. Zille improved the support base to 16.6 per cent in 2009 and, in the 2014 polls, pushed the figure up to 22.2 per cent.[1]

The real test of whether the DA has made the right choice in Maimane is due on 3 August 2016 – just 15 months after his election as leader. These local government elections look set to be a watershed moment, coming at a time of unprecedented public dissatisfaction with President Jacob Zuma following the Constitutional Court's ruling on Nkandla which found that the President's failure to implement the remedial action proposed by Public Protector Thuli Madonsela was 'inconsistent' with what is required of him as President by the Constitution.

Prior to the court ruling, Zuma and his cabinet had spent close to two years refusing to implement Madonsela's recommendations – chief among which was a call on the President to pay back a portion of the hundreds of millions of taxpayers' rands spent on 'upgrading' his private Nkandla homestead.

Still reeling from the news of the unanimous Constitutional Court judgment, the public was to soon hear the Supreme Court of Appeal rule that it was wrong for the National Prosecuting Authority to drop over 700 counts of corruption and fraud against Zuma in 2009. This ruling opened a possibility that, if the NPA decides to reinstate the charged, the country may go to the 2016 local government elections with the Head of State as an accused.

In addition, the President's ties to the controversial Gupta family had come under intense public scrutiny after deputy finance minister Mcebisi Jonas publicly revealed that members of the family, as well as the President's son Duduzane, had irregularly offered to make him finance minister. This revelation led to a number of other ANC politicians and senior government officials speaking up on how the Guptas had attempted to unduly influence them, apparently with the President's blessing.

As a result of an internal ANC fallout over these issues, and growing public anger over Luthuli House's refusal to act against its President, the ruling party looked set to enter the election race limping. The leaders of the opposition parties smelt blood and decided to exploit the controversies to their advantage. Immediately after the Constitutional Court delivered its damning verdict against Zuma, the Cabinet and the National Assembly, Maimane petitioned Speaker Baleka Mbete for an impeachment debate. Predictably, the debate ended with the ANC's numerical strength in the National Assembly ensuring that Zuma remained in office. But the DA had achieved its objective: it had shown up the ANC as a party that protects its leader at all costs even when the courts had made devastating findings about his conduct as head of state.

However, public anger over Zuma does not necessarily translate into massive new votes for elections. This is especially true during the local government elections, when local issues and candidates tend to be as important as the national political discourse, if not more so. It is conceivable that many traditional ANC supporters who are not happy with Zuma's continued stay at Mahlamba Ndlopfu will still vote for ANC candidates on election day.

For Maimane and the DA, however, there could not be a better time to head for the polls.

• • •

'WHERE WE GOVERN, WE GOVERN BETTER'

Even before Maimane's election as leader, the DA had set itself the target of winning more metro councils and other municipalities outside of the Western Cape where it is in charge of Cape Town and the majority of local governments. The crown jewel this time is to be the Eastern Cape's Nelson Mandela Bay Metropolitan Municipality, which is made up of Port Elizabeth and surrounding areas.

In Gauteng, given the dip in ANC support from 64.42 per cent in 2009 to just over 54 per cent during the 2014 general election,[2] the DA also has reason to believe it will do better in some of the province's metros come 2016. In the 2009 general elections, it won 21.86 per cent of the votes in Gauteng. Five years later, with Maimane as candidate for the premiership, that percentage had climbed up to 28.52 per cent. Now the focus is on the ANC's loss of support in the three Gauteng metros, where it used to command an unassailable majority. During the 2014 elections, in Tshwane, home to the country's executive capital, Pretoria, the ANC saw its share of the votes decline to 49.31 per cent, while its power in Johannesburg was reduced to 53.63 per cent. The party managed to win 56.41 per cent of the votes in Ekurhuleni. All of this, coupled with the fact that Gauteng accounts for 24 per cent of registered voters and that, in 2014, the party received more votes in this province than it did in the Western Cape, makes DA strategists see it as the next frontier.

According to Patricia de Lille, the 2016 local government elections were a major consideration when Zille decided on the timing for her stepping down as party leader. Zille had apparently started talking to trusted senior party leaders about the possibility of stepping down in September 2014, just a few months after helping the DA consolidate its position as the official opposition in the National Assembly. 'She was saying it is best to leave now and let a new leader prepare for the 2016 local government elections. She felt 2015 was enough time to give the new leader. My advice to her was, in politics, there never is a right time,' said De Lille.[3]

The party took a deliberate decision to hold its 2015 federal congress in Port Elizabeth to show that it was serious about taking the metro from the ANC. In his very first speech as DA leader, Maimane made it clear that he saw winning the Nelson Mandela Bay metro as 'one step closer to the Union Buildings'.[4] In the months that followed, he was to spend more weekends campaigning in the metro than he did in other parts of the country outside of Gauteng and the Western Cape.

When I asked him once why the metro was important for the DA to win, he said it was important that the party won more metros to show the electorate that 'where we govern, we govern better'. He went on: 'It is also symbolic. This is a city named after Nelson Mandela. There are eight metros in the country and the DA runs only one. If we win here and become government in two other metros, it means by the time we get to 2019 voters will be able to have a fair comparison of what happens where we govern as opposed to the areas governed by the ANC.'[5]

With the ANC having dropped to 48 per cent of votes during the general election in the area in 2014, Maimane was confident that the DA would emerge as the new government after the 2016 elections. Addressing hundreds of party supporters in the crime-riddled northern suburbs of Port Elizabeth late in 2015, Maimane dismissed those who were pessimistic about the party's chances of winning the metro: 'When we said we will win Cape Town [in 2006], they said "never, even the ancestors will punish you …". We took Cape Town and today even the ancestors in heaven are smiling,' he concluded in one of his rare moments of Zuma-style populism, skilfully mixing traditional and Christian beliefs to win over certain segments of the voting population.

In 2011, Zille had put a lot of effort into winning the metro and had banked on the Congress of the People performing well enough for the two parties to form a coalition government. However Cope's internal problems, emanating largely from a power struggle between founders Mosiuoa Lekota and Mbhazima Shilowa, resulted in the party winning just 6 out of the 120 council seats on offer. The DA obtained 48 seats while the ANC narrowly won the metro with 63 seats.

Athol Trollip, the man tasked with winning the metro for the DA, was confident that there would be no repeat of 2011 in 2016, even with the ANC having deployed SA Football Association supremo Danny Jordaan as mayor. 'The ANC won the metro by just over 50 per cent the last time. It won it in penalty shootouts. It is vulnerable and after the elections what we would see is the transfer of power,' he said.[6]

Trollip had just finished a tour of 60 wards over a period of 59 days when I interviewed him. What he saw in terms of the metro's failure to deliver basic services, he said, convinced him that the ANC was set to lose even more voters in the 2016 election. The city's public transport system was dysfunctional as the metro had spent R2.5-billion on a Bus Rapid Transit System that had not got off the ground. Drug-fuelled gang wars were the order of the day, especially in the northern suburbs, as there were not enough police on patrol. If he became mayor, he promised, he would form a working partnership with the City of Cape Town to learn how the latter had reduced criminal gang activities on the Cape Flats.

Trollip, who is also the DA's federal chairman and speaks fluent isiXhosa, is a popular figure among DA supporters in the city. Whenever he is about to deliver a speech at the party's township rallies, organisers introduce him with popular 1980s group Juluka's 'Impi' song. If Juluka's Johnny Clegg is the 'the White Zulu', Trollip is seen as *'umXhosa omhlophe* – the White Xhosa', in these parts. But if one of the reasons for choosing Maimane as DA leader at national level was the belief that he will attract the black voters the party needs, why not in Nelson Mandela Bay – a predominantly black municipality?

Trollip does not think that the race of a candidate is a key determining factor for performance at the polls. At one of the rallies he even quoted Chinese leader and reformer Deng Xiaoping's famous saying: 'It doesn't matter whether the cat is black or white as long as it catches mice.'[7] He is supported in this view by DA MP Ian Ollis, who believes that, unlike in countries such as the United States and Nigeria, South Africans vote according to their political party allegiance, rather than for individual candidates.[8] 'If the candidate was so important in South Africa, the people who voted for Mandela in 1994 would not be voting for Zuma today,' he said. 'In Nelson Mandela Bay people have been voting for the DA; there is a long tradition of more people shifting their allegiance to the DA with every election. We were already around 40 per cent in the last election and Athol and Mmusi would probably add another 5 per cent.'

But if the DA's best scenario in the metro is to get 45 per cent, where are they going to get another five plus one to be able to form a government? Trollip insists that they are aiming for an outright majority. But if that were to fail, they would go into coalition with the smaller parties, which he expects to do well at the polls.

Smaller parties, most of which were formed after breaking away from the ANC, pose the greatest threat to the ruling party as it prepares for the 2016 polls. The potential of such parties inflicting serious damage to the ANC's chances of holding on to a metro that was once home to struggle heroes such as Govan Mbeki and Raymond Mhlaba was dramatically demonstrated in the small and impoverished PE township of Veeplaas. Here, the ANC used to win every election without much effort. But an internal ANC power struggle in the region saw Veeplaas local boy and former National Union of Metalworkers of South Africa unionist Zanoxolo Wayile being booted out as metro mayor in 2013. This split the ruling party's support base. When a by-election was held, the ANC lost the ward to Bantu Holomisa's United

'WHERE WE GOVERN, WE GOVERN BETTER'

Democratic Movement. The UDM's votes grew to 49,5 per cent in the ward from a previous election showing of just over 1 per cent.

An embarrassed ANC spokesman, Zizi Kodwa, who had been among a group of senior ruling party leaders sent to the ward just days before the by-election to win back support, blamed the loss on his party's arrogance and complacency: 'You hear our people walking around [in the ward], for example, saying "this ward belongs to the ANC". No place in this country is guaranteed for the ANC. We've got to work hard for people's votes.'[9]

The UDM celebrated the victory, its first in the metro and one of the few in the Eastern Cape, by slaughtering 10 cows and 30 sheep for its rejoicing supporters.[10]

Trollip hoped that the same scenario would play itself out in other ANC wards in 2016. He specifically pinned his hopes on the EFF, which had not shown any serious presence in the Eastern Cape before the elections, and the United Front – a political vehicle formed by Numsa and other former Cosatu activists disgruntled with the ANC. If neither the ANC nor the DA won more than 50 per cent of the votes at the polls, he would work with the UDM, EFF and the likes of the United Front to form a coalition government.

But the ANC is not taking the fight lightly, spending much of its energy and resources after November 2015 trying to win back the residents' confidence in it. Several national government projects, including the multi-billion rand Operation Phakisa on the Oceans Economy, have been launched in the city by President Zuma. In a move reminiscent of 2009, when the ANC pulled out all stops to have a successful election rally in East London amidst indications that Cope had seen that city as its base, the ruling party decided to hold its 2016 election manifesto rally in PE.

The ANC's renewed endeavour to keep the metro under its control is not the main stumbling block to the DA's ambitions, however. Trollip's race may be a non-issue in his campaign to become mayor, but incidents of alleged racism within the party in Nelson Mandela Bay region have the potential of weakening his chances of victory. In June 2013, long before Trollip was declared a mayoral candidate, a DA councillor, Stanford Slabbert, shared a racist e-mail authored by someone else with his colleagues in the council. The e-mail, which was supposed to be a criticism of Zuma's leadership, stated that South Africa had become 'the race capital of the world' and a country 'where the president has more wives than actual brain cells'.[11] It further stated that 'the country that gave the world Dr [Chris] Barnard and various leaders' now only produced 'dumb idiots who wait for handouts'.

The DA fired Slabbert and stripped him of his party membership. Speaking as the party's provincial leader, Trollip said Slabbert's actions were 'contrary to the values of the DA and are condemned in the strongest manner'. But despite the party having acted, its detractors are using the e-mail as a campaign tool, telling Port Elizabeth residents that voting for the DA would be voting for the return of apartheid.

Trollip's attempts to distance the party from the e-mail were not helped by accusations that in July 2015 another DA councillor, Chris Roberts, had called a colleague, Mongameli Bobani, '*Bobbejaan*', Afrikaans for baboon. Roberts denied the accusation but was later fined R10 000 by the party. He resigned as a whip but kept his seat as a councillor. His continued membership of the council was criticised by the ANC and a former DA councillor, Knight Mali, who said it proved that the party was not serious about fighting racism within its ranks.[12] It was clear by then that, much as the DA in the metro hoped to hurt the ANC at the polls by capitalising on its internal divisions and accusations of corruption, the ANC was equally determined to use charges of racism to discourage voters from seeing the DA as an alternative.

So what if the DA fails to win the Nelson Mandela Bay metro after Maimane and his team have put so much emphasis on taking it over: will it lead to a rethink about him as leader? Probably not, but everything depends on how the party performs in the other metros and municipalities it has targeted, especially in Gauteng. There, Tshwane is the lowest hanging fruit, following the ANC's failure to garner more than 50 per cent of the vote in the city during the 2014 polls. The DA won 38 per cent while the EFF, which was participating in the elections for the first time, received 10 per cent of the votes in the metro. The remainder went to smaller opposition parties. Had those polls been for local governments, the capital city would have fallen to opposition hands.

Various polls and studies show that the ANC's losses in Pretoria are largely due to young voters turning their backs on the party. This is one of the regions in Gauteng where the EFF is said to be strongest.

To ensure that the party performs better than the 38 per cent it received in 2014, Maimane and the DA are fielding a fairly young Gauteng MPL, Solly Msimanga, as their mayoral candidate. Born in 1980, Msimanga is one of those party activists Maimane will have to rely on in the coming years as he strives to turn the DA into a party of choice for the youth. Trained in marketing, Msimanga grew up in Pretoria with very little interest in politics. Then one day, after studying the branding strategies of various political parties, he decided to write a letter to DA leader Tony Leon, telling him that he did not resonate with black people and needed to change.[13]

That letter led to a meeting with then DA chief strategist Ryan Coetzee and, later, Zille. Soon thereafter, Msimanga was part of a team responsible for the party's rebranding. He later obtained a scholarship to study politics as part of the DA's Young Leaders Programme. This saw him being sent to the Friedrich Naumann Foundation, the German-based organisation that promotes liberalism, for short courses. When Maimane was chosen as the DA's mayoral candidate for Johannesburg in 2011, Msimanga was the party's operational director, ensuring that the campaign proceeded smoothly from the administrative side of things. Later that year he became a councillor in Tshwane, a position he held until he became an MPL in 2014.

Like Maimane, Msimanga is a devout Christian and an elder at the United Reformed Church in Pretoria.

That the contest for Tshwane would be fierce was clear to Msimanga soon after his nomination as mayoral candidate. Late in 2015 he and Maimane were scheduled to address an election rally at Solomon Mahlangu Square in Mamelodi Township, east of Pretoria. The square, named after ANC guerrilla Solomon Mahlangu, who was hanged by the state for his uMkhonto weSizwe activities in 1979, is one of the busiest parts of this vast township over weekends. Having a rally there meant that the DA would be able to reach out to thousands of residents who pass through the square as they go about their weekend business. But when party organisers arrived at the venue on the Friday to prepare for the weekend event, they were prevented from branding the square with the party's paraphernalia on the grounds that it was to be used for a 'student prayer meeting'.

A group of youth, believed to be Cosas members, arrived at the scene and started telling DA activists that they were not going to allow 'people responsible for Mahlangu's killing' to set up camp there. Stones were thrown; fire extinguishers were used to chase the DA supporters out of the venue, and some of them had their T-shirts torn, said Msimanga. Metro police refused to help, he added. The whole saga was later to be a subject of a civil suit.

To Msimanga what the incident indicated was that the ANC 'realised that it was losing power' in the city. 'A dying horse kicks the hardest,' he said. That things were changing in Pretoria could be seen by ordinary residents' reaction to the DA, he added. In the past there was much hostility and it was 'regarded as taboo' to wear a DA T-shirt. 'Now people invite us to their community meetings and want to hear what we plan to do differently.' At one ward in Soshanguve, north of Pretoria, the DA used to score no more than one per cent of the votes, but when by-elections were held in the area in late 2015, the party had grown to 40 per cent: 'They are starting to see us as the alternative. Unlike in the past, our biggest branches now as the DA are in the townships.'

Msimanga believes that Maimane's election as DA leader has helped change people's perceptions of the party: 'It has taken out this propaganda that the DA is a white party. People are now seeing young, black and dynamic individuals in leadership positions. We are now turning the narrative and telling our own story.'

Msimanga did not rule out any coalition with other parties if the DA failed to win an outright majority in Tshwane. However he warned that the party would not enter into any agreement in which it was a 'junior partner' because 'to deliver on our promise we need to determine the direction the city takes'. Given that the ANC was the only party likely to garner more votes than the DA if none of the parties wins more than 50 per cent of the vote, it was clear from his statement that Msimanga would not be interested in co-operating with the ruling party.

By late October 2015, informal talks between the EFF and the DA had started on how the two parties were going 'to safeguard each other's interests' during the election campaign period.

• • •

If Msimanga, the lesser known of the DA mayoral candidates for the various metros, is the most likely to deliver a victory for the party in Gauteng, paradoxically it is the most famous candidate who looks most unlikely to succeed.

Herman Mashaba is, without a doubt, one of the most celebrated black entrepreneurs in South Africa today. The story of how he started his haircare products company, Black Like Me, in 1984 at a time when the apartheid system discouraged the rise of black industrialists, remains an inspiration to many. A staunch believer in the free market system, it is perhaps no surprise that Mashaba – who was critical of the ANC's economic policies as far back as the early 1990s – would find a political home in the DA.

What was surprising was that the DA, with its strategy to win Johannesburg by growing its following among middle-class black voters, would choose him as a candidate. With his conservative views on the country's labour legislation, BEE and affirmative action, Mashaba is more likely to appeal to the DA's traditional constituencies than to attract legions of new ones. In the weeks and months following his selection as the DA's candidate, Mashaba has seemed to fare better with the callers on predominantly white radio stations than on black ones. Although the interviews have generally been about what he plans to do for the city if he becomes mayor, they have generally ended up being about national government policies – largely because that is what seems to have driven him into politics.

A few months before the announcement that he had been selected as the DA's mayoral candidate, Mashaba participated in a Young Professionals Debate organised by Ollis at one of the top Sandton hotels. On the panel with him were Maimane and a veteran liberal journalist, Denis Beckett. Although Mashaba and Maimane consider each other as good friends, it was clear from the engagement that they hold conflicting views on a number of fundamental policy issues. Whereas Maimane supports a form of affirmative action that does not impose strict racial quotas because 'there is strength in having diverse places of work', Mashaba believes such corrective measures to be unnecessary and discriminatory against white people: 'If this country's economy was growing at 5 per cent year on year, it does not have enough whites to fill all the jobs. Ultimately the economy, the free market, determines,' he said.[14]

When a young black professional in the audience questioned Mashaba further on his statement, he said: 'I raised it to make the point that we don't need legislation to address race. We just need to focus on growth.'[15] He holds similar views on BEE, which, he said, leads to business people 'being harassed on a daily basis' by government agencies 'who want to confirm if I am black or not'. Maimane, on the other hand, sees the need for policies aimed at 'including those who are excluded' from mainstream economic activities. This, he said, must include support for micro enterprises because 'we are out of balance because we only just depend on big business, not that it is bad, when ultimately micro enterprises drive economic growth'.

For Mashaba, the country's labour legislation is the sole cause of high unemployment as it takes away employers' power to determine what they want to pay for labour: 'One thing that is unfortunate about our country is that we created a notion that people are exploited. Exploited by whom? I worked for Spar and they paid me R105 a month. I exploited Spar within seven months to attract more opportunities ... We need to build another culture in the country that says "guys, go out there and exploit business".' Maimane was cautious, telling the audience to understand historical exploitation and that some of the laws were there to protect the most vulnerable: 'I have been to places where you find people working in environments that are not suitable for human beings,' he said. While Maimane suggested that the country's fundamental problem was not its policies, but the poor quality of leadership at the helm which creates policy uncertainty, Mashaba believed the country needs a complete overhaul.[16]

With views like these, Mashaba was always going to rub large sections of the black middle class – many of whom complain that transformation in the workplace has not happened fast enough – the wrong way. Yet his candidature has its up-sides. Due to his public profile, he has attracted much media attention and therefore helped keep the DA's electoral campaign in people's minds.

• • •

Maimane's success in his first major test as DA leader will not only be determined by which new municipalities the party wins, but whether it is able to keep its traditional stronghold in the fold. 'As much as we want to go up in Tshwane, Johannesburg and Port Elizabeth, we should never take voters for granted,' says Cape Town mayor Patricia de Lille. 'We must work hard to retain Cape Town, Midvaal and the other municipalities we control.'

When he became party leader, Maimane stressed the need to retain Cape Town, with its reputation as the best-run metro in the country, as the city that would make the party attractive to voters dissatisfied with the way their local governments are run. Although Luthuli House has in the past stated that it is keen to win back the city it lost to Zille in 2006, it has made no real effort to take the fight to the DA. Instead, the ANC's leaders in the province have been too consumed by their intra-party conflicts to stage any daring attempt at taking over Cape Town.

As the DA leaders pointed out above, becoming part of government in two or three other metros would give the party about three years, before the 2019 general election, to build a compelling case for the argument that where the DA governs, it governs better than the ANC. Controlling more metros could also go a long way to dispel public fears, especially among the poor, that a DA government would mean a return to a form of apartheid and the scrapping of social grants.

If the takeover of more municipalities comes via the creation of coalition governments in municipalities where there would have been no outright winner, this may hasten the process of 'political re-alignment' that the DA has been talking about since Zille became leader in 2007. This realignment may not involve the EFF, as the ideological platforms of the two parties clash sharply. But it may see the tactical alliance that has existed in Parliament between the DA and the EFF spread to local government levels.

CHAPTER 7

Jousting against the red berets

THERE WAS A TIME IN SOUTH AFRICAN politics when conversations about the future were dominated by speculation over which of the ANC's politicians was likely to end up as the country's president in future. It was a period in which the liberation movement-turned-governing party's electoral dominance was unassailable and opposition parties appeared too weak and meek ever to pose any serious danger to its hold on power. If there was ever to be any threat to the ANC, analysts predicted, it would come in the form of a split within its alliance, with socialists in Cosatu and the SACP breaking away and the ANC becoming more centrist.

The prediction of a neat break-up along the assumed ideological lines never came to pass. But even as the ANC's internal leadership battles exposed irreconcilable fissures that were beginning to develop into insoluble contradictions by the mid-2000s, Jacob Zuma's claim that the ANC 'will rule until Jesus comes' did not seem to be too far fetched. Back then, the names of ANC heavyweights such as Joel Netshitenzhe, Jeff Radebe, Nkosazana Dlamini-Zuma, Cyril Ramaphosa, Saki Macozoma, Trevor Manuel and Pallo Jordan were on most commentators' lips.

Those who cast their eyes beyond the 2019 general elections looked to an even younger generation and started speculating about former ANC Youth League presidents Malusi Gigaba and Fikile Mbalula as likely future candidates for the Union Buildings. These two had played significant roles in the movement that helped Zuma win political power in 2007. But by 2012, ahead of the ANC's Mangaung conference, Gigaba and Mbalula were on opposing sides of a bitter leadership battle that saw Deputy President Kgalema Motlanthe challenge Zuma for the party leadership.

Gigaba backed Zuma's bid for re-election and his name was initially put down on the pro-Zuma election slate as the faction's candidate for the position of ANC deputy secretary-general – a strategic stepping stone to the presidency. He was later dropped, with Zuma campaigners opting for Jessie Duarte as the most suitable candidate for that post. Gigaba's removal from the 2012 slate derailed his presidential ambitions by more than a decade, if not permanently.

Mbalula, on the other hand, had thrown in his lot with the Motlanthe campaign and was nominated by this faction for the post of ANC secretary-general. Motlanthe lost the presidential race to Zuma while Mbalula was defeated by Gwede Mantashe in the battle for the secretary-general post.

Had Motlanthe and Mbalula won the respective posts, it is highly likely that the former would have been in charge of the party until December 2022 and that the latter would have succeeded him as party leader and head of state. But they didn't and, as South Africa approached the end of Zuma's turbulent tenure, the immediate leadership succession planning centred on Ramaphosa, who took over from Motlanthe as deputy president, ANC treasurer-general Zweli Mkhize, National Assembly Speaker Baleka Mbete and former African Union Commission chairperson Nkosazana Dlamini-Zuma.

Whereas smart money is still on the ANC winning the 2019 general election, albeit with a reduced majority, the ongoing trend of the party shedding more voters with every election means that it can no longer be taken for granted that the ANC will be able to form a government on its own come 2024. It is therefore no surprise that speculation over who is likely to become president in future is no longer limited to ANC politicians. The names of two opposition leaders are often brought up during discussions: Mmusi Maimane and Julius Malema.

The belief that the ANC will not be able to win over 50 per cent of the votes in 2024 is very prevalent within DA ranks, with most citing internal leadership strife, which they assume will continue long after Zuma has stepped down, as the reason for their optimism. As DA shadow minister of human settlements Makashule Gana said: 'My observation is that the ANC will start disintegrating as there will just be a lot of internal fights for positions. As a result, their supporters won't come out to vote and there will be an upswing in the number of people voting for the opposition.'[1]

As leaders of the DA and the EFF, Maimane and Malema would be the biggest beneficiaries if such an ANC disintegration were to continue. To varying degrees, they both owe their status as leaders of the country's two main opposition parties to the collapse of the ANC's internal cohesion post-Polokwane. When they qualified to vote for the first time in 1999, both men voted for the ANC, and probably did the same in 2004. In the Zuma presidency era, and for totally different reasons, the two found themselves in the opposition ranks, fighting the ANC.

Although in Parliament the two parties have often co-operated – especially in the campaigns to force Zuma to account for Nkandla and to commit to responding in person to MPs' questions in the National Assembly as per the rules – they are both aware that they are in fierce competition for votes. Hence their relationship inside and outside of the legislature has been both hostile and friendly. At a personal level, the two leaders of the opposition get on well – so well that when Malema was about to get married, he personally invited Maimane to the wedding as one of his guests.[2] The DA leader, however, could not make it to the wedding due to prior commitments.

The cordial personal relationship also made it easy for the two parties to work together in uniting the opposition on issues of common interest, such as when they demanded that Zuma resign following damning findings against him by the Constitutional Court. But both recognise that they are essentially fishing in the same pond for votes and that having too close a relationship could harm both brands.

The EFF has positioned itself as a leftist and radical African nationalist organisation set up to fight the 'neo-liberal' policies of the governing ANC. Its 'revolutionary' credentials cannot be enhanced by a close association with the DA – a party Malema has always rejected as a parliamentary shop steward for 'white monopoly capital'. The DA, for its part, sees the EFF as 'ANC lite'[3] and believes that the party's 'populist policies' – which include the nationalisation of mines, banks and other major industries as well as land restitution without compensation – would ruin the economy.

At the heart of their differences is not just ideology, but the fierce battle for the disaffected black voters they each need to grow into a serious alternative to the ANC. In the 2014 elections, the DA won just over 4 million votes, about 50 per cent of which came from white voters. The other half was from coloured, Indian and black voters. What was most significant for the DA about that election, the last to be fought under Zille's leadership, was that about 750 000 of those votes were from black voters.

This meant that the DA was now the third most popular political party among black voters, a few hundred thousand votes shy of matching the EFF, which secured over a million votes, the majority of them from black voters. Maimane's election as DA leader meant that the party's energies would now be devoted to expanding its support base within this constituency, something that both Malema and the ANC would have seen as a potential threat.

Just days after Maimane announced that he would avail himself as a candidate for the position of DA federal leader following Zille's announcement that she was to step down, Malema went on the offensive: 'I think Mmusi can make a very good principal; he is not a politician,' he said. 'We are over the moon as the EFF because we won't have serious competition from Helen to Mmusi. It's now us and the ANC and I think we'll take it from here.'[4] He also told reporters at another event that he was worried that if Maimane won the DA leadership race, he 'will turn the DA into a church': 'Politics don't need pastors. They need politicians. The DA is going to be converted into a church,' Malema said in reference to Maimane's other role as a pastor.[5]

Malema's dismissal and ridiculing of Maimane as a worthy adversary sought to hide his worry over a new kind of DA, one that could no longer be easily scoffed at as a 'white people's party'. With Maimane, his peer and a black leader, in charge, Malema knew that he would now have to contend with more than the ANC as he tried to position the EFF as the party of choice for black youth.

Even as the two worked closely in Parliament in 2016 in the bid to force Zuma out of office, Malema was still portraying Maimane as an unworthy opponent. A day after the DA held a relatively successful election manifesto launch at the Rand Stadium in Johannesburg, the first mass rally of its kind for them, Malema was in Ebony Park in Midrand telling supporters to ignore Maimane because he was not in charge of the DA: 'Don't be misled by the DA. The DA has two leaders. It's Helen Zille and Mmusi Maimane. Mmusi is used to attract black voters; the real leader is Helen Zille who is the white leader of the DA.'[6]

Although Maimane's approach since becoming DA leader has been to see other opposition parties less as adversaries and more as partners in the struggle to reduce the ruling party's dominance, he has had his choice words for the EFF. In July 2014, two months after he and Malema became members of Parliament, Maimane told the Cape Town Press Club that the EFF leader was a hypocrite and a populist whose ideas were irrelevant and unworkable: 'It remains to be seen what the EFF is going to do, and whether or not there will be constant reporting on the wearing of red overalls and domestic worker uniforms to Parliament,' he said.[7] (At the time, the EFF was still the flavour of the month in Parliament, grabbing public attention away from the DA and other opposition parties through its unusual dress code and combative approach to parliamentary debates.)

In late 2015, with the DA's internal figures showing that the EFF's potential support among voters had doubled to about 12 per cent nationwide[8] while the DA's had remained stagnant at around 25 per cent, Maimane again took a hardline position: 'We don't stand for the same things,' he said when asked if the DA would consider forming a coalition with the EFF in municipalities with hung councils after the elections. 'I think the better coalition would be between the ANC and the EFF because they believe in the same things, effectively.' He considered himself to be in competition with 'the ANC/EFF alliance' as the two parties 'are both drawing out of the same policy space' while the DA wanted to see alternative policies implemented.

Zille had held a similar view in the run-up to the 2014 general elections, stating categorically that the DA 'will not enter into a coalition with the EFF under any circumstances' as such a move 'would be unworkable' given the huge ideological gulf between them. She also saw the EFF and the ANC as 'two sides of the same coin'.[9]

Maimane put forward a set of conditions as the basis for any coalition with other opposition parties that made him seem unlikely to be interested in a formal relationship with the EFF, especially at national level. The DA, he insisted, would not enter into any coalition with any political party that 'mobilises on the basis of race'.[10] Given that the EFF's main message to the electorate is that it is a party fighting for the rights of 'blacks' who have been 'dispossessed' of their land and mineral wealth by 'whites', a coalition agreement ought to be ruled out between the two parties.

Maimane also said that his coalition partners would have to believe in the market economy, a condition that the EFF – which often flirts with socialist ideas – will certainly not accept. But this does not rule out the parties working closely together and forming tactical alliances in municipalities where joint efforts can lead to them unseating the ANC. This tactical alliance, albeit informal, already exists in the National Assembly where the two parties usually join forces on issues of mutual interest.

By the end of 2015, Malema was already showing willingness to cooperate with Maimane if this could help either of the parties grab a municipality or two away from the ANC. As he phrased it, 'I am saying to him: "Let's talk. Put what you are offering on the table and we'll also put what we are offering on the table."'[11]

• • •

Whatever happens between the DA and the EFF after the local government elections, one thing is for sure, the two leaders stand to experience very different personal outcomes as regards their chances of ever seriously contending for the Union Buildings.

The EFF is pretty much built around the personality of its leader, Malema, and he is unlikely to suffer any damage within the party if they perform poorly at the polls. Besides, for a self-styled revolutionary party such as the EFF, electoral politics is merely one 'terrain of struggle' and if the party fails there, Malema could redirect it into extra-parliamentary forms of mobilisation.

The situation is different for Maimane. He was elected to grow the party's share of the vote especially among young and black voters in urban centres. Failure to do so could leave him vulnerable to a successful leadership challenge by his opponents within the DA at the party's next federal congress. But if the DA does well in the 2016 elections and grows to beyond the 30 per cent mark in 2019, Maimane is likely to still be around in 2024, the year which he and other DA leaders believe will see the ANC's support among voters decline to less than 50 per cent.

Would he or Malema emerge as president then? Considering the DA's current electoral strength, as compared to the EFF's, and the fact that the party has been growing with every election, at face value Maimane seems to stand a greater chance than Malema. Whatever he lacks in terms of Malema's larger-than-life personality, he compensates for by being in charge of a party with strong organisational structures that extend to most parts of the country. These structures mean that the DA has a far greater capacity to canvass for support beyond its strongholds, while the EFF has zero presence in rural areas and smaller towns, especially in the Eastern Cape, KwaZulu-Natal, Mpumalanga and Free State. Maimane has further strengthened the DA by insisting that party activists are visible on the ground where they interact with communities. Since he came into power, the party has run door-to-door campaigns canvassing for support on a weekly basis. He has been leading from the front, criss-crossing the country almost every Saturday and Sunday in search of new members and supporters. Although his EFF counterpart does the same often, his visits appear to be limited to specific areas where the EFF has strong support.

Malema clearly has his sights on becoming South Africa's president one day, and is not satisfied with merely being on the opposition benches. Since entering parliamentary politics he has been quietly trying to clean up his public appearance by shedding his 'bad boy' image while retaining the persona of an uncompromising radical. Before his expulsion from the ANC, he had gained a reputation among his critics as an 'ignorant' ANC Youth League president who could not even pass woodwork at matric. Since then he has returned to school, acquiring a university degree, and has slowly repositioned himself as something more than a rabble-rouser, namely a leader with an alternative vision for South Africa.

He has addressed a number of international platforms, indicating that even the outside world no longer dismisses him as the 'buffoon' many seemed to think he was when he first burst onto the national stage declaring that he would 'kill for Zuma'. But this does not mean that his politics has now become universally appealing. There are still many voters, both black and white, who are put off supporting the EFF because of its calls for the nationalisation of mines and the repossession of private white farms by the state. There are others, however, especially the unemployed youth, students and young black professionals who feel marginalised by the system and see in the EFF a party that represents their aspirations.

However history does not seem to be on Malema's side. For all its fascination with talk of revolution, the South African body politic has proven over decades to be conservative and more receptive to parties that espouse centrist policies. Throughout the battle against colonial domination and apartheid, the centrist ANC always had leftist and more radical opponents to contend with. But these – from the New Unity Movement in the 1950s to the Black Consciousness Movement in the 1970s, and not forgetting the Pan Africanist Congress – never grew to pose a real challenge to the centrist party's dominance. In the democratic era, most parties to the left of the ANC have struggled to win more than a per cent of the votes. The EFF, with its 6 per cent in the 2014 elections, has been the most successful of this cohort of parties.

But if the leftist EFF cannot effectively challenge the ANC, can a

JOUSTING AGAINST THE RED BERETS

Maimane-led centrist DA do it? Listening to DA supporters at party rallies, you'd be convinced the answer is in the affirmative. At such rallies, Maimane is often introduced as 'the president in waiting' or 'South Africa's next president'. The party's leaders, however, are more cautious. Ollis, for instance, believes that what Maimane will manage in the next few elections will be to grow the party from its current 4 million votes to 6 million. (The ANC won the last election with over 11 million votes.)

• • •

In his first year as DA leader, Maimane appeared to have done enough to convince his party's supporters and members that he could take on Zuma and the ANC both inside and outside Parliament.

While the EFF and Malema succeeded in turning the Nkandla scandal into their campaign issue, Maimane's DA effectively used Parliament to challenge the President, the executive and the ANC on a broad range of issues. Where the parliamentary process failed them, Maimane has not been shy to approach the courts. He took Parliament to court on several occasions to challenge National Assembly Speaker Baleka Mbete's decisions.

According to De Lille, the courts have become an important instrument for holding Zuma's executive to account. 'That is Maimane holding government to account. We get accused of taking everything to court, but that is what the courts are there for ... Mmusi must also be measured by the number of cases we have taken to court and won.'

The DA has indeed gained a reputation as a litigious political party. But the one case the party decided not to take directly to the Constitutional Court is the one that mattered most. When Parliament decided to set up a process to conduct its own investigation into whether the R246 million spent on security upgrades at Zuma's Nkandla home was justified, the DA and the EFF objected to the process on the grounds that it undermined the work already done by Public Protector Thuli Madonsela. However the DA decided to participate in the process while the EFF boycotted it.

When the final report, which cleared Zuma of any financial liability, was finally tabled before Parliament and voted on, the EFF threatened to go to the Constitutional Court. The DA, which already had two other cases before the courts relating to Nkandla and the Public Protectors' powers, initially refused to be part of the matter because it was not convinced that the EFF would succeed in its bid to approach the court directly. It was a tactical mistake, not a fatal one, but one that would hand over victory to Malema on an issue that the DA had led for years.

Maimane, however, was able to gain some lost ground after the groundbreaking judgment that found both the President and Parliament had failed to uphold their constitutional obligations. He reacted by calling for Zuma's impeachment. Although the Speaker readily agreed to the impeachment debate, Maimane and the DA took a lot of flack from commentators who accused them of wasting time as they knew they were never going to win the vote. With 62 per cent of the seats in the House, the ANC was guaranteed an easy victory. To impeach the President, Parliament needs two-thirds of MPs to vote in favour.

Maimane's critics correctly pointed out that the DA had called for similar votes and debates in the past only for the ANC to rally around its embattled leader. Others suggested that by calling for the vote, the DA was prolonging Zuma's stay in power as ANC members would have no option but to defend their President from opposition attacks. But what they seemed to miss was the DA's reasoning behind this strategy. The party was well aware that it was not going to win the vote. However, by forcing the vote on the matter, Maimane and the DA succeeded in drawing the ANC into the saga. It was a clever move, one that would be used during the DA's election campaign to tell voters that the problem was not just with the unpopular Zuma, but with the rest of the ANC whose MPs chose to back him despite the court ruling.

• • •

But what of Maimane when Zuma is gone? It is relatively easy to be an opposition leader when your adversary is a scandal-prone president who happens to have over 700 possible charges of corruption hanging over his head.

In 2019, if Maimane runs for president, it will not be Zuma that he will be up against. He is likely to be running against Cyril Ramaphosa or Nkosazana Dlamini-Zuma, both seasoned politicians with relatively good reputations in the eyes of the general public.

Maimane's recurring message since joining the DA in 2011 has been that the current ANC is 'no longer the ANC of Nelson Mandela' and other anti-apartheid struggle icons. Under Zuma, he has often argued, the ruling party abandoned its principles and values. The implication of this argument to some voters may be that there is nothing wrong with the ANC, just its leader, and that once he is removed from office, the party will be back on track. Such logic can't do the opposition much good.

To succeed he will have to devote his efforts to presenting a different version and plan to the electorate, policies that speak to how the DA plans to reduce unemployment and growing levels of inequality in society.

CHAPTER 8

An end to ideology?

BUT WHAT DOES MAIMANE STAND FOR? What does he believe in? Is he a liberal, a Christian conservative or a believer in supposedly illiberal African philosophical notions such as ubuntu? These are questions that have dogged Maimane and his backers ever since he gained national prominence following his appointment as DA national spokesman and his selection as the party's candidate for the Gauteng premiership ahead of the 2014 elections.

His questioning on various policy issues reached fever pitch around April 2015 as it became apparent that he would be Zille's successor despite a challenge from former academic and respected DA MP, Wilmot James – considered by some to possess superior liberal credentials.

The leadership contest came a year after Zille's attempt to attract more black voters by parachuting in her then friend and former boss, Mamphela Ramphele, as the DA's presidential candidate spectacularly backfired when the latter pulled out of the deal at the eleventh hour.

Ramphele, who had started her own political party, Agang SA, in 2013, had initially agreed on a deal that was to see her name topping the DA's

AN END TO IDEOLOGY?

parliamentary candidates list and members of her new party formally joining the official opposition party. But a few days after she and Zille announced the pact, she reneged, apparently because of opposition from Agang members who did not want to be incorporated into the DA.

Announcing the collapse of the deal, Zille said the 'historic partnership' would have led to the creation of a 'strong and united alternative to Jacob Zuma's ANC'. 'People are looking for a strong and united alternative to Jacob Zuma's ANC, and we felt that Dr Ramphele would help us speed up the realignment of politics.'[1]

The failed move indicated that, despite having grown the DA's support among voters since taking over in 2007, Zille believed that she was about to reach the ceiling and that for the party to break through it, they needed a black leader. Ramphele ticked all the right boxes. Not only was she black, a former University of Cape Town vice-chancellor and an ex-World Bank managing director, she had impeccable 'struggle credentials' – having been one of the founders of the Steve Biko-led Black Consciousness Movement of the 1970s.

In post-apartheid South Africa, Ramphele had stayed out of party politics, preferring instead to concentrate on business and academia. For years, Zille revealed in her press statement announcing the collapse of the deal, the DA leader had 'sought to bring her into politics' and the two of them went 'through many false starts' before Ramphele finally agreed to join forces with the DA.

City Press reported that the first official meeting between Ramphele and a DA delegation led by Zille took place on 18 August 2012 at the Villa Belmonte in Cape Town.[2] Several others were to follow at which the two parties discussed how they could best work together. At some stage the parties even agreed to form a new political party called The Democrats, which was to be a merger between the DA and the constituency that Ramphele promised to bring with her.

The new party was to be announced in February of the following year and was supposed to be officially launched on Youth Day, 16 June 2013. By early 2013, however, the negotiations had collapsed and Ramphele had announced the formation of her own party, Agang SA. But Zille persisted as she was very keen to have her on board and had already made up her mind that she was going to step down as DA leader after the 2014 elections.

Cape Town mayor Patricia de Lille was one of the DA leaders closely involved in the talks with Ramphele. She said that after Agang had been formed, the two parties returned to the negotiating table and by the beginning of 2014 it seemed as if a deal had been clinched.[3] The DA would name Ramphele as its presidential candidate and she, in turn, would fold her party into the DA. But then, five days after the announcement was made, Ramphele pulled out of the deal, causing a disappointed Zille to say her party had the values, structures, machinery and 'depth of leadership to succeed' without Ramphele.[4]

De Lille believes that Agang's formation complicated matters, as some of the people who had joined the organisation saw it as a vehicle for them to be MPs and would not accept a merger with the DA as this meant their chances of going to Parliament would be reduced. Some of them had come from other opposition parties and had joined Ramphele convinced that, unlike the leaders of parties they came from, she had the kind of political pedigree that would make the majority of voters dump the ANC and vote for her to be president.

De Lille thinks that those individuals pressured Ramphele not to take the deal, convinced that she would do well on her own. 'When you open a new bar all the drunks kicked out of other bars come to the new bar. That is what happened with Agang. I saw a couple of people that left the ID [the Independent Democrats – the party De Lille led before it folded into the DA] who were now with Agang. These people were not happy that she was now joining the DA.'[5]

AN END TO IDEOLOGY?

Although De Lille believes that Zille's attempt to bring Ramphele over enjoyed universal support among DA leaders, others say they were not convinced from the onset that Ramphele was the solution to the party's problem of attracting black voters. Party MP Makashule Gana said that while he supported the idea of a black leader and understood the argument that, because she was already a brand on her own, Ramphele would bring more votes, he thought they were going about it the wrong way. 'She was someone who was once a prominent leader and we now wanted to repackage her and present her as new. What South Africa needed was a new generation of leaders, a new generation of freedom fighters and not the old one.'[6]

At the time of the talks, Maimane never publicly shared his views on Ramphele becoming party leader. But in his BBC HARDTalk interview just two months after being elected DA leader, he intimated that 'the decision to bring her on board ... was just wrong. We are proving, certainly by my own election, that there can be organic growth and that we can arrive at a point where we can elect a candidate who comes from the party and we can build diversity.'[7]

Ramphele's decision to walk away, as well as Lindiwe Mazibuko's departure to Harvard University soon after the 2014 elections, paved the way for Maimane to become DA federal leader. But that is not to say the position was handed to him on a platter. James gave Maimane a decent contest even though the latter ended up winning comfortably by getting close to 90 per cent of the votes.

On a few occasions the contest between the two groupings took a nasty turn. In one instance, an anonymous e-mail was circulated among DA leaders and journalists alleging sexual misconduct on the part of individuals associated with the Maimane campaign. The e-mail was dismissed as part of a smear campaign and its author never attempted to substantiate the claims. In another alleged 'dirty tricks' incident, some party MPs said to be opposed to Maimane's ascension to the top job tried to get Parliament's ethics committee to investigate if he had not breached the rules by allegedly not declaring his involvement with a certain company. The allegations were later proven to be false.

But on the whole, the contest between Maimane and James was conducted in a positive spirit. The two politicians made history when they agreed to a public debate, just days before the federal congress, on how each planned to take the country forward. This was the most high-profile political television debate between two politicians vying for office since the pre-election debate between ANC President Nelson Mandela and the National Party's FW de Klerk in 1994.

Besides being the first of its kind in the democratic era, the debate – broadcast on the Afrikaans TV network kykNET and moderated by *Rapport* editor Waldimar Pelser – revealed much about the often under-reported political differences of opinion that exist within the DA.[8] Because of the ANC's sheer size and the amount of political drama it generates, little attention is often paid to opposition parties and the ideological fissures playing themselves out within them. Hence much of the change that has occurred within parties such as the DA, as they grapple with how best to position themselves to challenge the ANC's omnipotence, goes unnoticed and the contradictions that emanate from that are ignored.

For most commentators, James fared much better than Maimane in the interview on crucial policy questions, even though he did sound unconvincing in his answer on whether rape accused have a right to bail. James had caused much controversy a day earlier when he told the *Sunday Times*'s Chris Baron that he believed that bail should not be granted to people accused of rape. When Pelser pointed out to him that this stance sounded more populist than liberal and could possibly be against what is enshrined in the Bill of Rights, James re-stated his position: 'Bail is not punitive ... What I would recommend is that the default position in violent crimes is no bail unless the accused and the defence can make a case for bail to be granted.'

Maimane objected to this stance, pointing out that there were 'many people who have had allegations against them' and their constitutional rights should be protected even if they are accused of the serious crime of rape because they were innocent until proven guilty.[9]

If Maimane came across as a firm believer in the Bill of Rights and James seemed to favour a more populist approach, the two were to exchange positions on the next question. Did Maimane support calls for the holding of a referendum on the death penalty and on same-sex marriages?

'If the people want to vote on it, the people must vote on it,' said Maimane, later adding that 'the ultimate right given to the people of this country is that it must always be their voice that must be given expression'. Personally, he added, he would not support the death penalty because he understood 'that our judicial system still has flaws' but 'ultimately as a democrat' he upheld the people's right to vote on the matter.

'What happens if the views of the people clash with that which is enshrined in the Constitution?' asked Pelser.

Maimane responded by saying he did not believe that would happen as 'many South Africans will believe in the protection of the Constitution'.

His comments drew a sharp response from James: 'I think Mr Maimane doesn't understand our Constitution at all ... The Bill of Rights, which has the right to life ... cannot be changed by a vote in Parliament, it cannot be subject to a referendum.'

In the hours and days to come, James's supporters would use Maimane's responses to support their charge that he was not fit to lead a party with such a strong liberal heritage as the DA, as he was not liberal enough. In one interview, James went as far as to suggest that what Maimane wanted to do was to turn the DA into another version of the ANC where liberal values would not be central to the party's beliefs.

Stung by the accusation, the Maimane campaign hit back, questioning James's own credentials as a long-standing liberal.[10] Maimane's campaign manager Geordhin Hill-Lewis issued a statement in which he stated that James, in an interview five years earlier, when he was already a prominent DA MP, had said he would vote for the ANC if it had former finance minister Trevor Manuel as its president.[11] 'Indeed, James worked closely with the ANC throughout the 1990s and would later describe himself in an interview as an ANC sympathiser during those years,' Hill-Lewis wrote in the press statement. He also pointed to James's involvement with the Black Consciousness Movement of the 1970s as well as the ANC's internal wing – the United Democratic Front – in the 1980s. 'He was never a member of the Democratic Party or any of its predecessor parties and only joined the DA in August 2008 – a few months before he became an MP,' said Hill-Lewis (without pointing out that, as a coloured person, James would have been prohibited from joining the 'predecessor parties' due to racist policies of the time).

For obvious reasons, Hill-Lewis's statement also concealed Maimane's own past sympathies for the ANC.

James responded by accusing Maimane of using Hill-Lewis as a proxy to fight him: 'If Mmusi Maimane has something to say about this issue then he should have the courage to say it himself, rather than hiding behind a proxy.'[12] He was not the only one to chastise Maimane for suggesting that a referendum on the death penalty and gay marriages may be permissible. Commentators in the mainstream media, as well as social media, admonished him.

A day after the debate, Maimane took to Facebook to complain that 'some people' are 'distorting my position on gay rights'.[13] 'As I said last night: "I still stand on the view that gay rights must be protected. South Africans who are gay and want to marry each other are entitled to do so. The law gives that right, so I don't know what the referendum would be about. In fact, I still maintain that those rights are in the Constitution and must be protected".

But DA supporter and young gay rights activist Siya Khumalo was one of scores of others who were still unhappy. He wrote on his blog that 'Maimane's understanding of constitutional democracy and the fundamental rights of individuals is what's distorted. In his worldview, South Africans are nearly unanimous in the understanding of the indivisibility of the Bill of Rights (the world must be pretty through those rose-tinted spectacles); they are so constitutional and liberal and democratic, he says, that their power to infringe on the rights of others shouldn't be infringed upon; the referendum should happen so as to show that South Africans support the democratic principles of the constitution by which they democratically received a voice, he's telling us.'[14]

Maimane was also to come under fire for comments he made during a sermon at Liberty Church in 2014 in which he appeared to be saying that gays and Muslims were sinners. In the sermon, he said of his work as a 'missionary' of God's kingdom: 'Me, I really wanna be a friend of sinners. That's part of the mission that I believe God has given us, to be a friend of sinners. Because, you know what, I am a sinner. So I guess we can be friends, right? But I don't want to just be their friend 'cause I want them to think, I'm like, they are like a project. I want them to sincerely know I'm their friend. So, you know what I am most grateful of, is that in my friendship circles there are Muslims, there are gay people – because I believe that is what God has called us to do. I take the verse that Jesus says, "I didn't come for the well but I came for the sick". I take that quite seriously.'[15]

As the storm grew, Maimane tweeted a picture of himself at a same-sex civil union and wrote: 'I have always supported gay rights & always will.

We're all equal. I celebrated my friend's wedding as a witness'.[16]

During the kykNET debate, Maimane's commitment to liberal values also came under scrutiny when Pelser asked him if, as a Christian and a pastor in his church, he believed God spoke to him about how to lead the party in Parliament. He did not directly respond to the question: 'It's important, it's my own choice … I still maintain my faith … It's something I must practise – I am entitled to do so.'

Maimane then complained about a 'generalised view' that if you have a religion 'you cannot be liberal'. This was dangerous, he said: 'I think the issue here is that I have a personal conviction … but I also understand that my faith is subject to the laws of the country.'

Maimane's complaint about the 'generalised view' that religious individuals – especially those who belong to Pentecostal Christian churches – cannot be trusted with upholding the liberal values enshrined in the Constitution was not without merit. When Zuma appointed Mogoeng Mogoeng as Chief Justice in 2011, one of the greatest grievances against him expressed by critics was that he was a lay preacher at a local branch of the Winners' Chapel, a Nigerian-based conservative Christian church opposed to gay marriages, the right to choose and other rights protected in the South African Constitution.

Yet since taking office, Chief Justice Mogoeng – who was also accused of being a Zuma lackey – has not written any judgment that suggested that he put his faith above the Constitution and the country's laws. Instead, he has over the years come to be seen as one of the greatest champions of the country's supreme law, especially following his reading of a groundbreaking and unanimous Constitutional Court ruling ordering Zuma and the government to comply with the findings and recommendations of the Public Protector on Nkandla.

But given the fact that Maimane's association with the Liberty Church, which also holds socially conservative views on a range of issues including homosexuality and the possession of pornographic material, causes his critics to question his suitability for the DA leadership, I asked the man who recruited him to the party if he considered him liberal.

Ian Ollis, who is openly gay, regards himself as a classical liberal who is proud of having come 'from the Progressive Federal Party side' of what later became the Democratic Party, before being renamed the Democratic Alliance. He would not give a categorical answer on whether he considered Maimane a fellow liberal.[17] However, he did say that when Maimane appeared before a selection panel to choose the DA's mayoral candidate for Johannesburg in 2011, he gave liberal answers to questions.

Ollis was a member of the panel, and although he had a major hand in bringing Maimane to the party, he still had to ask him tough political and leadership questions to assess if he would be the party's best candidate for mayor. 'Well,' he said, 'I am not allowed to reveal what is said in the internal election processes and debates ... I asked him questions in the selection panel ... and he generally picked liberal answers on abortion and gay rights. So I am not concerned. He believes in democratic rights, liberal rights and in the Constitution ... There are other people in the party who I am concerned about, who I don't think are liberals.'[18]

Writing in *The Star* newspaper ahead of Maimane's election as DA leader, columnist and social commentator Eusebius McKaiser confessed that he 'warmed my liberal heart' with his answer to a question on the decriminalisation of sex work during an interview the two had. 'Maimane thinks sex work should be decriminalised, and even regrets some of the ways in which the DA government in the Western Cape responds to sex work and sex workers. It ought to be entirely one's own choice whether or not one wants to sell sex for monetary compensation, and the law shouldn't police one's choices on this matter.'[19]

But does Maimane consider himself a liberal? He clearly does, especially when one looks at his broadly liberal attitude towards a market economy and the country's Bill of Rights, which is based on liberal values. However, liberalism, he has argued, is constantly evolving and has to be redefined to respond to local conditions: 'Every ideology defines itself in a space and a time and a context,' he says.[20]

Like Zille before him, Maimane hardly uses the term in his DA speeches, causing purists to view him with suspicion as someone who would betray Helen Suzman's legacy. But an honest assessment of the DA's origins shows that it has never been a 'pure' liberal party. The party came about in 2000 as a result of Tony Leon's Democratic Party merging with Marthinus van Schalkwyk's National Party. As author and commentator Songezo Zibi points out in his book, *Raising the bar – hope & renewal in South Africa*, the vast majority of the National Party supporters who joined the DA had never believed in liberalism but supported apartheid policies and opposed Suzman's liberal views in the old whites-only parliament.[21]

The merger did help the party to grow, especially among Afrikaans speakers and coloured and Indian voters who previously voted for the National Party. But it also meant that DA policies shifted rightwards and towards conservatism on issues such as minority rights and the need to redress past imbalances that were a legacy of apartheid. Although Van Schalkwyk later broke away from the DA and collapsed the New National Party into the ANC, after securing important government positions for himself and a few others, the huge majority of former National Party voters remained with the DA.

Just how influential some of these former Nats remained in the DA long after Van Schalkwyk's departure was evident in a piece penned by Maimane's predecessor as DA leader in Parliament, Lindiwe Mazibuko.[22] Responding to Maimane's efforts to root out racism within the party, she wrote of a culture where 'the liberal credentials of former National Party members are never questioned' in the same way that their black counterparts are called 'the black caucus' and 'illiberal racial nationalists'.

After Zille took over the DA leadership, the party further consolidated its hegemony within the Cape coloured constituencies by absorbing De Lille's Independent Democrats. The DA, under Zille and Maimane, has been preoccupied with growing its electoral base by attracting more black voters disgruntled by the ANC. Many of those former ANC supporters converting to the DA would not be doing so because they found liberalism as an ideology attractive, but because they were looking for a viable alternative to the ANC.

Susan Booysen, a professor at the School of Governance at Wits University, has argued that the DA is faced with a choice of 'three futures'. The first is to be a growing party that remains predominantly liberal but without the 'added momentum that could allow it' to catch up to the ANC. Alternatively it can reposition itself to 'become more like the ANC in policy and ideology', 'offering a cleaner, less corruption-prone party'. The third option is 'largely suspending prior ideology' to become 'a vote-catching party machine' that is willing to align itself with other parties to form governing coalitions.[23]

Maimane appears to favour a more pragmatic approach that avoids an ideological straitjacket. He once asked on Twitter if the country had 'not entered an era of post-ideologism' and answered his own question thus: 'Philosophically that can't be, but pragmatically that could be so.'[24]

De Lille, who describes herself as a social democrat, agreed with the 'post-ideology' assertion. 'Before 1994, contestation was ideological. It ended post-1994 with the adoption of our Constitution. For anybody today to say De Lille is not a liberal, it does not make sense. It has no meaning and adds no value. The only ideology now is our Constitution.' What is the definition of a liberal, she asked rhetorically. 'Even if he [Maimane] was not one, so what?'[25]

Even Ollis, a diehard liberal who once proposed a motion at the party congress that future recruits be educated on the DA's 'set of liberal values,'[26] does not believe it matters to voters. Unlike voters in Europe, locals worry more about jobs, crime, education and housing than they do about ideology.[27] 'Helen stopped using the term, she took liberal out of her speeches and the reason for that is that South Africans don't understand it. You have to explain it in simple terms, like freedom of religion and women's rights. That is why I can't see future leaders of the DA speaking all the time about liberalism ... But I would be very angry if future leaders of the party do not support liberalism.'

Voters' apparent inability to understand the concept of liberalism is unlikely to be the only reason it is used sparingly by the DA as it seeks to increase its support among voters. In the interview referred to above, Maimane told McKaiser that he did not think it 'made tactical sense to bang on about the word' liberal as it 'was divisive inside and outside the party'.[28]

As academic Merle Lipton points out in her 2007 book, *Liberals, Marxists, and Nationalists,* resentment is widespread especially within the black intelligentsia and middle class. Diplomat, academic and former activist in the liberation movement, Eddie Maloka, has argued that this hostility stems from South African liberalism's origins in the nineteenth-century Cape Colony 'as an adventure of a handful of whites determined to protect white minority interests in a colonial setting'.[29]

Former cabinet minister and ANC thinker Pallo Jordan has been more nuanced in his criticism of early South African liberalism, acknowledging the positive contribution of slavery abolitionists such as Thomas Pringle and William Porter while criticising their support for a qualified franchise that excluded most black citizens of the Cape Colony. He wrote: 'South African liberals' split personalities can be traced to the decades preceding the opening up of the mines in 1867. Their humanism persuaded a man like Pringle to raise his voice against racism, slavery and colonialism. But the liberals were also integral to the colonial settler society and saw their future within. Thus were the majority of liberals tempted to expediently compromise principle when it clashed with the interests of the empire.'[30]

This track record did not improve following the formation of the Union of South Africa in 1910, as most liberals continued to believe that a universal franchise 'was too radical'. 'Running like a blue thread through the history of South African liberalism is a readiness to defer to White prejudices,' charged Jordan.[31]

Jordan's criticism of the South African liberal tradition extends beyond 1994. He was once quoted saying that the DA 'adopted the tattered garments of white anxiety … appealing to the worst fears of white voters and becoming rather illiberal'.[32] But defenders of the liberal tradition such as Lipton and Michael Cardo, author of legendary Natal liberal Peter Brown's biography, *Opening men's eyes*, denounce the vilification of 'liberalism as a mere adjunct of imperial conquest, racial segregation and capitalist exploitation'.[33] Cardo points to the active role Brown and other members of the Liberal Party played in opposing apartheid and how the party had black members until it was forced to disband in 1968, following the promulgation of the Prohibition of Political Interference Act. This piece of legislation prohibited blacks and whites from belonging to the same organisation.

Before its disbanding, the Liberal Party had begun supporting universal suffrage.[34] Cardo points out that at its 1961 conference, the majority of Liberal Party delegates attending were black. 'The Liberal Party was not a party for minority interests. It was not beholden to big capital. And it understood that liberalism is not just about formal equality alone.'[35]

However the DA's political roots are not in the Liberal Party, but in the Progressive Party – a whites-only liberal party formed in 1959. Unlike Brown's liberals, the Progressives supported a 'qualified franchise' for blacks and refused to participate in extra-parliamentary protest actions aimed at undermining the apartheid state. Over the years the Progressives' political tradition became the most dominant of the two South African liberal tendencies through the Progressive Party's successors – the Progressive Federal Party, the Democratic Party and the DA.

It is partly due to this complex history that, even though the vast majority of South Africans agree with most liberal values enshrined in the Constitution, they remain suspicious of the ideology. While arguing that liberals should take on board 'informed criticism' of their historical role in South African politics, Cardo believes they should not allow this to be used to discredit the ideology. He seemed to agree with the approach the DA had increasingly taken under Zille and Maimane when he urged liberals to 'find ways of accommodating diversity and addressing poverty while gaining the momentum of political support'.[36]

In an interview a retired Brown gave in 1996 shortly before his death, he predicted that there would 'come a time when the ANC starts to disintegrate or to produce factions' and that this 'will be an opportunity to form a fully non-racial Liberal Party again'.[37] He envisaged this party as 'something which will absorb' the DP 'and elements from other political organisations'.[38] A decade after Brown's prediction about the ANC, the ruling party did indeed start to disintegrate and, by the time Maimane became leader of the DA, it had suffered two major splits – losing millions of voters in the process.

• • •

Is Maimane going to advance the South African liberal tradition, albeit in a moderated form, and help it move from the periphery to the centre of local politics?

Even though it is the oldest modern tradition in South Africa, having been imported to the country by nineteenth-century European migrants to South Africa, liberalism has never been a dominant political ideology in the country. It struggled to compete with both Afrikaner nationalism and African nationalism throughout most of the twentieth century; even Marxist ideology fared much better in winning the hearts and minds of South Africans during the struggle against apartheid.

But that is not to say that its principles and values were rejected. In fact, for most of the struggle against apartheid, they found expression more in the organisations that had taken to extra-parliamentary opposition to apartheid than those who professed themselves liberal.

Maimane may have to draw lessons from all of those – from Peter Brown, Selby Msimang and Helen Suzman right down to liberation struggle leaders with liberal leanings such as Nobel Prize winner and ANC president Chief Albert Luthuli.

CHAPTER 9

Dress rehearsal for the main event

The Rand Stadium occupies a special place in the history of racial segregation in football. Nestled between mine dumps in Rosettenville, south of Johannesburg, the stadium was first opened in 1951 as a 15 000-seater facility. In the years preceding South Africa's isolation from international sport due to its apartheid policies, it hosted games involving such European soccer household names as Real Madrid, Ajax Amsterdam, Arsenal and Newcastle United.[1]

By the early 1970s, apartheid South Africa was under sustained pressure from the International Federation of Association Football (Fifa) to drop the racist policies that prohibited athletes from different racial groups from playing together. To dissuade Fifa from banning its member associations from sending teams to South Africa, sport and recreation minister Dr Piet Koornhof announced that the government had approved 'the staging in 1974 of an open national soccer tournament in which different South African nations can participate on a multinational basis'. This meant that 'a South African representative white team, a South African representative Zulu, Xhosa or any other Bantu national team can compete in the tournament'.[2]

DRESS REHEARSAL FOR THE MAIN EVENT

The whites-only South African team played its black counterpart twice at the Rand Stadium later that year. The black team lost both matches, 4-0 and 3-1. A similar competition, known as the Embassy Multinational Series, was also played at the stadium with the whites-only team winning 2-0.

It was at the same venue in 1975 that the then whites-only Cape Town-based Hellenic beat what would later become Maimane's favourite soccer team, Kaizer Chiefs, to be crowned winners of the Chevrolet Champion of Champions. Koornhof again had a hand in this tournament, permitting that it be organised as a competition where 'white and non-white clubs could take part'. The cup final was played over two legs, with Hellenic winning the first leg in Cape Town 4-0 and Chiefs winning the return leg 2-1. Although Chiefs lost the cup, their 2-1 victory at Rand Stadium was celebrated as 'the first win by an African team over a white one'.[3]

When the DA chose the Rand Stadium as the venue for the launch of its 2016 local government election manifesto, it is unlikely that the foregoing history would have played any part, though the party puts a lot of thought into matters like the choice of venue when organising such big events. Ahead of the 2014 national elections, for example, the party chose the Polokwane Showgrounds in Limpopo to send a message that its support among black voters was not confined to large urban centres like Johannesburg and Cape Town.

In 2011, battling to fight off the stigma of being labelled a party of apartheid that would drag South Africa back to the dark old days of racial discrimination, the DA took its launch to Walter Sisulu Square in Kliptown, Soweto – the birthplace of the Freedom Charter. Explaining this decision in a DA newsletter at the time, national spokesperson Lindiwe Mazibuko said the DA intended to show the electorate that it was a party 'that remembers the events of South Africa's difficult past' and that 'we will never forget the sacrifices that were made' to secure liberation. 'But we are also a party of the future, and our future lies beyond the municipalities of the Western Cape … With a foothold in government in two other provinces (Gauteng and the Eastern Cape), Johannesburg – and Soweto in particular – symbolises the next frontier for the DA,' she wrote.[4]

Holding the rally at the square angered the ANC, whose spokespeople accused the DA of trying to steal the legacy of anti-apartheid heroes and ANC icons like Walter Sisulu and to claim association with the Freedom Charter, a document rejected by the DA's predecessors as a socialist pipe dream.

It was this desire to capture more votes in Gauteng that drove Maimane and his team to take the 2016 rally to Johannesburg. With his eyes on causing a major upset by reducing the ANC's majority to less than 50 per cent in Tshwane and Johannesburg, Maimane knew that the launch rally could not be held anywhere else. But the choice of venue had another purpose: to send a strong message that, under Maimane, the DA is a growing party, especially among black voters.

Since its inception in 2000, the party has chosen modest venues for its rallies, not believing that its supporters would come out in big numbers. This has been changing slowly since Zille became leader. Now they were going to have an election rally at a soccer stadium that seats 30 000 people. It was a big gamble, especially because the rally was to be carried live by all the 24-hour news channels and other television stations.

A week before the DA rally, the ANC suffered a public relations disaster when its promise to fill the Nelson Mandela Bay Stadium with 100 000 party faithful failed to materialise. Instead rows of empty red seats left many without doubt that there were hardly 40 000 people at the venue. This further fuelled perceptions of an ANC whose popularity is rapidly waning and whose stranglehold over cities such as Port Elizabeth is weakening.

The DA could not afford to suffer the same fate, especially given the fact that its other rival, the EFF, was to hold its own rally a week later.

Mmusi Maimane (front row, first on the right) with Under-12 teammates at the Dobsonville-based Ontario Football Club. PHOTO COURTESY OF KGOTLA MOLEFE

Mmusi Maimane and his grandmother Lillian 'Elle' Morake. Mma Morake, as she was known in the neighbourhood, played an important role in Maimane's upbringing. PHOTO COURTESY OF THE DA MEDIA OFFICE

Maimane's parents Simon and Ethel with their daughter-in-law Natalie and son Mmusi at their home in Dobsonville, Soweto. KEVIN SUTHERLAND/GALLO IMAGES

Ian Ollis was instrumental in convincing Maimane to choose the DA as his political home. He is seen here with fellow party member John Moodey on 3 February 2012 in Johannesburg. SIMPHIWE NKWALI/GALLO IMAGES

A selfie Maimane took with Mbeki in Parliament ahead of the State of the Nation Address in 2013. MAIMANE'S TWITTER ACCOUNT

Mmusi preaching. PHOTO COURTESY OF THE DA MEDIA OFFICE

Mmusi Maimane and his wife Natalie at the opening of Parliament in Cape Town on 17 June 2014. The DA had just elected Maimane its parliamentary leader. NARDUS ENGELBRECHT/GALLO IMAGES

LEFT: The campaign bus Mmusi Maimane used as he canvassed for votes in his unsuccessful 2014 bid to become Gauteng premier. JONATHAN KATZENELLENBOGEN/AFRICA MEDIA ONLINE. RIGHT: Mmusi Maimane and Helen Zille addressing a press conference during a 2014 DA march to the ANC's national headquarters to demand the creation of jobs. GRAEME WILLIAMS/AFRICA MEDIA ONLINE

DA leaders, Helen Zille and Mmusi Maimane, during the launch of the party's Gauteng manifesto launch and job rally at Ellis Park Stadium on 29 March 2014 in Johannesburg. DENZIL MAREGELE/GALLO IMAGES

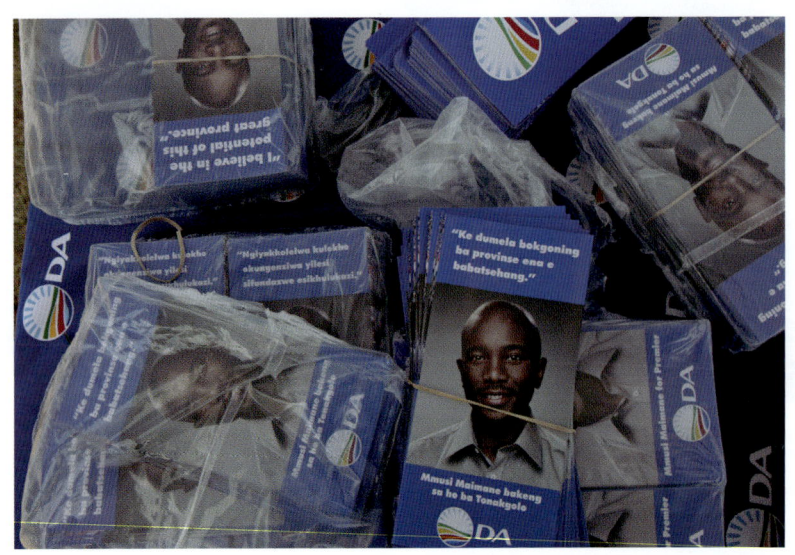

Mmusi Maimane campaign literature for handing out at a walkabout near Park Station in Johannesburg shortly before the National Election in 2014. JONATHAN KATZENELLENBOGEN/AFRICA MEDIA ONLINE

DA leader Mmusi Maimane casts his vote on 7 May 2014 in Soweto. This was the fifth democratic election in South Africa's history.
BONGIWE GUMEDE/GALLO IMAGES

LEFT: Former DA leader Tony Leon during an interview on 21 May 2014 in Johannesburg. LEON SADIKI/ GALLO IMAGES
RIGHT: Nelson Mandela Bay Metro mayoral candidate Athol Trollip. JONATHAN KATZENELLENBOGEN/AFRICA MEDIA ONLINE

Western Cape premier and former DA leader, Helen Zille, announcing that she would not be available for re-election as head of the DA in the next election on 12 April 2015. FELIX DLANGAMANDLA/GALLO IMAGES

Mmusi Maimane sings and dances during the DA's campaign on 6 April 2016 in Soweto. The DA continued their campaign ahead of the final registration weekend scheduled for 8 and 9 April 2016. FELIX DLANGAMANDLA/GALLO IMAGES

LEFT: Mmusi having tea with Archbishop Emeritus Desmond Tutu at the Desmond and Leah Tutu Legacy Foundation in Cape Town on 21 October 2015. RUVAN BOSHOFF/GALLO IMAGES. RIGHT: 'If you are racist, don't vote DA.' Mmusi Maimane addressing supporters on race and identity at the Apartheid Museum in Johannesburg on 19 January 2016. The address came shortly after the DA expelled Penny Sparrow from the party for calling black people monkeys and uttering other racist remarks. PETER MOGAKI/GALLO IMAGES

Outspoken DA MP Dianne Kohler Barnard who found herself in hot water after sharing a Facebook post that suggested South Africa was better under apartheid president PW Botha than under the ANC. MICHAEL HAMMOND/GALLO IMAGES

Deputy Public Protector, Kevin Malunga, and Mmusi celebrate on 31 March 2016 after Chief Justice Mogoeng Mogoeng ruled in a unanimous Constitutional Court judgment that President Jacob Zuma had to pay back the money for some of the upgrades to his Nkandla homestead. FELIX DLANGAMANDLA/GALLO IMAGES

Mmusi Maimane speaks in the National Assembly during the debate of a motion to impeach President Jacob Zuma on 5 April 2016 in Cape Town. Zuma survived the impeachment. ESA ALEXANDER/GALLO IMAGES

Mmusi Maimane during a march on 27 January 2016 in Johannesburg. DA senior leaders joined thousands of supporters in a march for jobs. MOELETSI MABE/GALLO IMAGES

Mmusi greets the crowd during his party's manifesto launch on 25 April 2016 at the Rand Stadium for the 2016 local government elections. SIMPHIWE NKWALI/GALLO IMAGES

LEFT: Mmusi (white shirt) speaks to the party's KwaZulu-Natal provincial leader Zwakele Mncwango on 3 May 2016 as they walk through an informal settlement while on the campaign trail in Durban's Clare Estate area. GIORDANO STOLLEY/AFRICA MEDIA ONLINE. RIGHT: Julius Malema, leader of the EFF, embraces Mmusi Maimane during the commemoration rally of the third anniversary of the Marikana massacre where 34 mine workers were killed by police. DEAAN VIVIER/GALLO IMAGES

DRESS REHEARSAL FOR THE MAIN EVENT

By mid-morning on Saturday, 23 April 2016, thousands of blue-T-shirt-wearing DA supporters were streaming into the venue singing about removing Zuma from power and Maimane taking over. They came from all over the country, but the majority were from informal settlements, townships and the inner-cities of Tshwane, Johannesburg and Ekurhuleni. The last time the stadium was fuller than that day was when Moroka Swallows beat University of Pretoria to win the 2009 Nedbank Cup soccer final.

Gone were the days when the DA's only association with the country's dominant pop culture was to play a CD of the late Brenda Fassie's nineties' hit, 'Vulindlela'. Now they had rap artists such as Ricky Rick, house music icon Liquid Deep and 2015 Idols winner Karabo Mogane performing at their rally. If Kwaito singer Chomee was the queen of ANC bashes, the DA had found her equivalent in up-and-coming performer, Bucie.

Granted, Rand Stadium is much smaller than the Nelson Mandela Bay Stadium. But the fact that the DA could almost fill up a 30 000-seater venue was a massive political statement, especially considering that the vast majority of those at the venue were young and black – a constituency that, only a decade earlier, hardly looked at the DA as a political alternative.

No longer could those black supporters attending DA rallies be dismissed, as was the case in the past, as 'rent-a-crowd'. Although mostly young, they were diverse in terms of social strata – suburban youth with Model C education sang side-by-side with the unemployed of Zandspruit and other informal settlements. This diversity was also reflected on stage with DA MP Makashule Gana, who looks and sounds like a township born-and-bred, as the master of ceremonies. The DA was sending a message to voters that it was not just a party of the elite.

But if Maimane's mission is to lead a truly non-racial party where individuals from diverse racial groups work side by side to build a better South Africa, that mission was not well reflected at the rally and many other DA mass gatherings before it. The crowd was almost exclusively black, despite the fact that close to 50 per cent of DA voters are white. As a result, when Maimane, at the beginning of his speech, said: 'When I look out at all of you I see the future of our country in all its glorious diversity,' his words sounded hollow.[5]

This gave ammunition to the party's detractors, some of whom started circulating on social media pictures of a predominantly white DA caucus in the National Assembly contrasted with the largely black crowds at party rallies and marches. Their message was clear – the DA's 'real' leaders were 'using' Maimane and other blacks in the party to gain more votes so as to keep their cushy positions in Parliament.

While it would be self-defeating of the DA leader to spend most of his time trying to prove to his political rivals that he is not a puppet, if he seeks to project the DA in the eyes of the general public as the most diversified party he has to insist that this be demonstrated in action.

In promoting his vision for South Africans to work together to build a better country, as stated in previous chapters, Maimane is fond of using the 1956 Treason Trial as testimony to the fact that this can be achieved. However the non-racialism of the 1956 generation was not limited to meetings in air-conditioned offices and conferences; it was also reflected in mass gatherings of the time. He has gone some way to addressing this, insisting – party insiders say – that DA members in Sandton should interact more regularly with their comrades in nearby Alexandra township. But this has simply not been enough to make the DA appear like the 'rainbow' party its leaders claim it to be.

Although he had been party leader for almost a year and had spent much of that period criss-crossing the country to promote the DA's Vision 2029, the manifesto launch was the first real opportunity for Maimane to present his case on a national scale. He used the stage to promote the DA as a party that defends the country's Constitution, contrasting this with the ANC whose President had recently been found by the Constitutional Court to have behaved in a manner 'inconsistent with the Constitution' when he refused to comply with the Public Protector's remedial actions on Nkandla.

'We must treasure this Constitution. It is the rock on which we must build our free and fair society. If we protect it, it will protect us,' he said.[6]

Once again he acknowledged that while 'apartheid may be dead and buried' its legacy lives on: 'And nowhere is this more evident than in the quality of education our children receive. Our poorest schoolchildren are being neglected, and the gap between the performance of poor children and the rich children is widening every day ... And half of our children don't even make it to matric, let alone pass. It is painful to say this but, two decades after the birth of our democracy, Bantu Education is alive and well.'[7]

The face of poverty was still black, he concluded, and, as a result of bad education, black people were falling behind other groups when it came to skills and jobs. In what was to be a recurring theme throughout the campaign – perhaps a retort to the ANC and EFF claims that the DA would 'bring back apartheid' – Maimane told the audience that the ANC 'governs as if black lives don't matter'.

The '#BlackLivesMatter' campaign began in the United States in 2015 following several cases of black youths being killed by white policemen in what were believed to be racially motivated incidents. By charging the ANC with governing 'as if black lives don't matter' Maimane was saying that there was no great difference between the ruling party and the actions of those 'racist' police in the United States. 'If you don't believe me, come with me to eGcuwa [Butterworth] in the Eastern Cape, where the local government spends millions on officials and politicians rather than on service delivery to the people. Here you will see people whose lives have come to a stop. There is no development and there are no job opportunities.' While South

Africans should never forget the damage caused by apartheid, they must be honest enough to accept 'that the last decade has been a missed opportunity to redress the legacy of our unequal past'.

It was an interesting statement, one that seemed to absolve the Mandela and Mbeki administrations from responsibility for all that has gone wrong. The blame, in Maimane's view, is all on the post-Polokwane administrations led by Zuma: '1994 brought the promise of change. And, yes, we made some progress. But in recent years we have started to go backwards. We have seen an increase in corruption, starting at the very top.'

The problem, of course, with this kind of reasoning is that it ignores the Arms Deal, Travelgate and other corruption scandals that have rocked post-1994 administrations. It also sends out a message to the electorate that the problem is not really with the ruling party or its policies, but with its current leadership.

Maimane and the DA seem not to have allowed for the possibility that, after its 2017 elective national conference, the ANC may emerge with a post-Zuma leadership that includes figures who worked closely with Mandela and Mbeki during the first three administrations of the democratic order. It would then be difficult for the official opposition to take on such a leadership if the DA's narrative is that South Africa had a golden era under Mandela and Mbeki.

Maimane also used the speech to take a swipe at the EFF, his direct competitor for the hearts and minds of young black voters who have turned their backs on the ANC. A few days before the DA's manifesto launch, Julius Malema had recorded an interview with Al Jazeera in which he threatened to use violence to remove the ANC from power if it employed state force to suppress opposition activities.

To clearly distinguish the DA from the EFF's politics, Maimane told the audience that it was up to 'a new generation of young South Africans to use political freedom to achieve economic liberation'. His message: 'When we take power, it will not be through the barrel of a gun. It will be the result of millions of South Africans coming together and casting their votes for change.'

• • •

It is all well and good to criticise the ANC government for its less than impressive delivery record on jobs, economic growth and corruption. It is easy to slam the EFF for its reckless militarist rhetoric and populist policy proposals. However, what does the DA offer to the voters?

For the local government elections, Maimane opted to use the DA-run city of Cape Town – the only metropolitan area the party controlled before the polls – to demonstrate the benefits of living in a DA municipality. Far from returning the city to the dark days of apartheid, the DA-led government had 'managed to increase the matric pass rate in the 21 high schools in Khayelitsha' – a predominantly black and poor Cape Town settlement – by 20 per cent in five years, he said.[8]

The city had also repealed over 300 outdated policies and by-laws that, among other things, made it difficult for the previously disadvantaged to create businesses in the city. 'Many previous policies were predicated on old apartheid laws that had never been repealed when the Metro was run by the ANC,' Maimane was later to say at a Cape Town rally.[9] The DA-run Western Cape, he added, has the lowest rate of unemployment in the country at 19 per cent. 'We run the best expanded public works programme in the country, with the highest number of jobs. Where the DA governs, jobs are created.'

For Maimane, small businesses are crucial in the drive to create jobs. His party has proposed that government's Black Economic Empowerment

Scorecard policies be amended to recognise small enterprises that create jobs: 'At present the socio-economic development element accounts for only 5 of the 100 points on the scorecard for generic enterprises. We propose an increased weighting for this element. We also proposed that points must be awarded in recognition of employment creation. Employment is the most sustainable way to lift people from poverty.'[10]

In Midvaal – the only Gauteng municipality under DA control before the 2016 elections – unemployment was the lowest in the province at 12 per cent, Maimane said. 'The DA has achieved this by making it easier for businesses to start up and survive in Midvaal. We have simplified by-laws and procedures ...'

A DA local government, he also promised, will invest in an effective public transport system that connects people 'to opportunities to work, learn and play ... We will bring bus and taxi transport systems to where they are most needed – in under-serviced communities ... We will make public transport easier by introducing a single "smart" ticket system so that commuters use just one ticket, be it for buses or taxis.'

• • •

As the country moves beyond the local government elections and begins to weigh its options ahead of the post-Zuma era, Maimane will increasingly be called upon to articulate his own plans for turning things around.

One concrete proposal he made during his first year in office was the reduction of the cabinet to just 15 ministries. He told the Cape Town Press Club on the eve of Zuma's 2016 State of the Nation address that reducing the number of ministries from 35 to 15 would save the national fiscus about R4.7 billion a year.[11] (Besides the 35 ministers, Zuma's executive also includes

37 deputy ministers – making it one of the largest in the world.) 'Let's be honest,' Maimane told the audience, 'our cabinet has become obscene. The staff, the bodyguards, the luxury cars, the first class flights ... All status, no substance and at the cost of billions of rands.' By 'cutting the fat', government would be able to reconfigure its ministries and departments 'with the single-minded objective of boosting economic growth and creating jobs'.

The size of the cabinet, Maimane argued, had a direct correlation with the size of the ballooning civil service wage bill which, by 2016, accounted for 40 per cent of government expenditure. His proposal was to reduce the size of the cabinet by scrapping some ministries and merging others while leaving the most essential untouched. If he were to be president soon, Maimane's cabinet portfolios would look like this:

Employment & Enterprise
Economic Infrastructure
Finance
Basic Education
Further Education, Skills & Innovation
Health and Social Development
Integrated Planning and Service Delivery
Police
Local and Provincial Government
Home Affairs
Agriculture and Land Reform
Justice and Correctional Services
Environment
Foreign Affairs
Defence[12]

The Employment and Enterprise ministry would be made up of trade and industry, small business development, economic development, mineral resources, tourism, and labour: 'This ministry would have one goal, and that is to grow jobs,' he said. His preference for a small cabinet, he explained, was based on the experiences of countries like Germany, which has 15 ministries, France, which has 16, and Brazil, which has an eight-member cabinet.

Maimane's critics say he does not do enough of this, presenting an alternative to how things are done by the ANC government. He is too comfortable banging on about Zuma and corruption within the ANC, the accusation goes. While railing against rising corruption in the public sector may win middle-class votes, political commentator Moeletsi Mbeki once argued,[13] it is worthless when trying to win over the poor: 'The DA seems to think it should go after the black middle class. They probably have quite a bit of that already. But they are barking up the wrong tree. The real target must be to increase its vote among the unemployed and the poor.'

If the party is indeed failing to attract the poor black voter, it is not for lack of trying. Many of Maimane's road-shows to promote Vision 2029 have involved visiting informal settlements and other areas on the periphery of the economy. DA activists such as Gana and Msimanga are quite active in black working-class communities and the outcome of several by-elections in areas such as Soshanguve and Mamelodi in Pretoria has shown that the party is steadily growing. However the competition is fierce. Not only do they have to contend with a firmly entrenched ANC in most of these areas, they also have to take on the EFF with its neo-leftist and, sometimes, Africanist, rhetoric that tends to easily find resonance with jobless youth living in squalor.

Maimane and the DA believe that campaigning for job creation policies helps them get through to this segment of the voting population. Their belief appears to be backed by the turnout in a number of marches the party has staged, especially in Johannesburg, to demand jobs. In January

2016 the party launched the Jobs Campaign by unveiling a billboard in the Johannesburg CBD with a ticker that counts the 744 people per day who lose their jobs under the Zuma administration. A march organised to mark the unveiling of the board was attended by thousands of unemployed people and DA activists.

Maimane's approach to tackling high levels of unemployment springs from the premise that it is not government's job to create employment. Its role 'is to create an enabling environment for job creation'.[14] This would entail state investment in public infrastructure, especially in transportation, communications and energy. It would also mean the introduction of other power-generating companies to compete with the state-owned Eskom. A DA government would also invest heavily in education, ensuring there is 'universal access to top quality schooling'.[15]

Over and above promoting the small business sector, which he argues creates more jobs than larger companies, Maimane wants to see current labour laws changed. 'Our current labour regime is not only hostile to investment, but simply unfair to the 8.3 million jobless South Africans in that it locks them out of the job market ... It is time to press the reset button on this one and introduce a new set of policies ... which create more opportunities for job seekers, by making it easier for businesses to hire; policies which promote excellence and competition and which give new entrants the opportunity to prove their willingness to work and learn.'[16] A DA government, he continued, would incentivise job creation through various schemes such as the establishment of special economic zones, tax rebates and promoting apprenticeship wages.

• • •

Much of the policy being proposed by the DA is rejected by the trade union movement, especially Cosatu, as tantamount to creating a two-tier labour system. But it is unlikely that this would concern the DA, as its focus is on winning over those who have been marginalised under the current labour system.

While winning support among the poor is essential for the DA, especially because they constitute the majority of the electorate, the black middle-class vote cannot be scoffed at. This is especially true in Gauteng, where the middle class constitutes 25 per cent of the electorate, and a substantial number of those defined as middle class are black.[17]

The black middle class, a by-product of ANC government policies – such as the Employment Equity Act – of the past two decades, has tended to be loyal to the ruling party. When the Congress of the People broke away from the ANC in 2008 following President Thabo Mbeki's recall from office, many analysts predicted that the black middle class would go with the party. Although Cope did get a million votes, most of this did not emanate from middle-class areas.

In the 2014 elections, however, the ANC in Gauteng blamed its heavy losses – which saw it decline by almost 10 per cent to settle at 54 per cent – on the black middle class turning its back on it.[18] Unhappiness with the ruling party over the imposition of e-tolls on the province's highways as well as government's handling of the controversy surrounding Zuma's Nkandla homestead ranked high among the reasons.

While some of these unhappy voters may have changed their allegiance to the DA and the EFF, the vast majority have decided to stay away from the polls. The EFF's radical policies, which call for the nationalisation of mines and banks, are not attractive to those in the middle class, who fear such policies may lead to Zimbabwean-style economic meltdown. But why not the DA; is it not their natural alternative? In many societies the middle class and professionals tend to be mostly centrist in their political outlook, so why would they be reluctant to follow a centrist party in South Africa?

Amuzweni Ngoma, an MA student in Sociology at the University of the Witwatersrand, did research on the subject and her article – 'Black professionals and the ANC' – was published in a book about the 2014 elections.[19] Ngoma argued that this noticeable reluctance on the part of black professionals to support the DA originated from its lack of clarity on Black Economic Empowerment. She quoted an economist who said they would have voted for the DA if the party was 'clearer on their transformation stance'.[20] (This must have been after Zille's 2013 fallout with Lindiwe Mazibuko over proposed amendments to the employment equity legislation, seen by some in the DA as 'imposing racial quotas'.) Even those Ngoma spoke to who said they were impressed by the DA's good governance record in the Western Cape still distrusted the party and saw Maimane and Lindiwe Mazibuko, who were the most visible black faces in the party at the time, as 'being used' by Zille.

Since taking over, Maimane has been trying to undo these perceptions and has used every platform available to express the party's support for BEE. 'I want to start by making it crystal clear that the DA unequivocally supports truly broad-based black economic empowerment. This is important because it is a widely held misconception that we do not,' he wrote in his weekly blog, *Bokamoso*, at the start of 2016. Measures to address the racial imbalances of the past were a 'moral imperative': the DA was committed to making South Africa 'a fairer society'.[21]

'An explicit BEE mechanism ... is the fastest way to unleash the massive untapped black talent and energy in our society and to unite us all around common interests,' the blog continued. Maimane disagreed with the view, prevalent among thinkers to the right of the ruling party and government, that empowerment should be 'poverty-based rather than race-based'.

'Understandably they wish to move away from using race in public policy,' he commented. 'But combating widespread poverty will not in itself succeed in helping black people to become successful entrepreneurs, or give them a stake in the economy.'

However the blog reveals that Maimane is critical of the current BEE system, saying it has not delivered meaningful empowerment in either scale or pace: 'This is largely because the system has been captured by a well-connected elite within the ANC that abuses it to become extraordinarily wealthy. So the same small group of beneficiaries are "re-empowered" over and over again, amassing incredible fortunes.'[22]

As a result BEE is not trusted by those not benefiting from the system. In its place, Maimane proposes a system 'that enjoys broad support from the majority of South Africans, black and white' – a tough ask, given that, by its very nature, BEE is an emotive issue that tends to divide rather than unite. But he thinks it can be done, firstly by empowerment scores awarding significant weight to employee share ownership schemes so that all employees in a company would have substantial ownership of the business. This, he argues, would at the same time grow black equity while encouraging productivity to increase. Having been given a stake in the company, the employees would then have to be represented at board level.

Maimane also believes that the scores should recognise money and time spent on improving staff members' skills and expertise as well as other forms of training. Government should reward companies that grow their work force through incentive schemes and give incentives to established businesses that help 'develop' new black entrepreneurs through direct mentoring and sub-contracting.

More controversially, Maimane believes that all small and medium-size businesses should 'be automatically classified as having the highest empowerment status', regardless of who owns them. 'This would effectively accelerate the growth of this sector, which has the combined effect of growing both entrepreneurs, innovation and most important of all, jobs.'[23]

Would this convince the black middle class, which is growing impatient with the slow pace of transformation in the private sector, that Maimane is serious about broad-based BEE and employment equity? Ngoma argued that many black professionals aspire to consolidate their class position and seek opportunities to move into an upper class. They see the ANC as instrumental in achieving this,[24] and may be unconvinced by a Maimane who says he supports BEE being race-based and then argues in the same breath that all SMME companies, regardless of race, should score empowerment scores for being small.

But what seems to count in his favour as the country gears up for the 2016 local government elections is the middle class's seeming determination to punish the ANC at the polls for sticking with Zuma even after the series of controversies that led to calls for his resignation.

Maimane was at the forefront of those demanding Zuma's impeachment, calling for the vote on the matter in the National Assembly. Although his party was inevitably outvoted, its actions won the support of those who were frustrated by the ANC's refusal to act against the President.

Since that debate, Maimane has wasted no opportunity to remind voters that, when given a chance, the ANC MPs refused to vote out Zuma from the office. The DA went so far as to compile a list of all ANC parliamentarians who voted 'to protect Zuma' and submitted it to Parliament's ethics committee for disciplinary action.[25] It was a gimmick, but one aimed at keeping the matter in the minds of the public as the elections approached.

But if the black middle class is unhappy with Zuma and wishes to teach the ANC a lesson, it is not a given that they will do so by voting for the DA.

Unlike in 2014, Malema is now a serious threat to both the ANC and the DA, having carefully used the EFF's presence in Parliament as the ultimate anti-Zuma. Despite winning most of the legal cases against the government and Parliament, including the 'spy tapes' case which may eventually lead to Zuma's corruption charges being reinstated, the DA has had to endure the EFF scoring a victory in the most crucial one – the Constitutional Court case over Nkandla.

Will voters see Malema as more effective in taking on the ANC and, therefore, give their votes to the EFF? The DA has at times appeared panicky over this, commissioning a helicopter to fly over the Orlando Stadium in Soweto with a DA banner while an EFF rally was in progress and sending out chain SMSes to voters demanding that Malema apologise for things he said and did while he was still an ANC member. All of this gives the impression that, far from its claim that there are 'only two bulls in the kraal', the DA is actually terrified by the EFF's growth.

Yet what Maimane needs to do is to concentrate on building the DA's reputation as the only party big enough to take on the ANC. He needs to remember that the local government elections are a dress rehearsal for 2019 and that he has to use this campaign to show sceptical voters that, under him, the DA has changed to become a party for all, that he is the man in charge, that he is no puppet.

Acknowledgements

One disturbing feature of the first two decades of democracy in South Africa has been the scarcity of black journalism voices in the discourse relating to the interpretation of the country's continuing transition and transformation. Black reporters may be at the forefront of breaking headline political stories for newspapers, radio and television stations, but are largely absent when it comes to recording that history, especially in book form. It was Professor Xolela Mangcu who remarked, just after former president Nelson Mandela's death, that despite the important role Madiba had played in bringing about a liberated South Africa, none of the scores of books about him is by a black scholar or journalist.

South Africa's painful history and the incredible change it has gone through since the early 1990s, as well as the challenges that lie ahead, cannot be fully understood without a diversity of voices that is reflective of our diverse experiences and interpretations. There are a variety of reasons – some say excuses – why there are very few current affairs books by black practising journalists. These range from lack of resources and the inability to take time off from a paying full-time job for research work to alleged lack of appetite from industry for such voices.

I am grateful to Jonathan Ball Publishers, especially Publishing Director Jeremy Boraine, for giving me the opportunity to add my own small voice to the ongoing conversation about the current state of our politics as well as its possible future.

This book would have been impossible without his patience and understanding, especially because I embarked on the project during a tough period when the *Sunday Times* was going through massive changes that demanded undivided attention.

I would like to thank my employers, Times Media Group – especially my former editor Phylicia Oppelt and current editor Bongani Siqoko – for allowing me time and space to work on this book.

Although Mmusi Maimane's busy campaign schedule meant that I was unable to gain the kind of access to him I had hoped for, the few occasions I interacted with him were invaluable. A word of appreciation, too, to his office for providing me with his full curriculum vitae as well as a schedule of his public engagements and political rallies.

I am also grateful for the help I received from Maimane's friends, colleagues and acquaintances – some of whom would not grant interviews but were kind enough to direct me where to go for the information I needed. Among them were individuals who had great admiration and deep respect for Maimane, but would not go on record because they belonged to a political party in competition with the DA and feared they might be accused by their comrades of 'promoting' an opposition leader.

My colleagues in the politics department at the *Sunday Times*, especially Sibongakonke Shoba and Jan-Jan Joubert, helped me with contacts as well as background information relating to some of the media reports about the DA's internal politics.

ACKNOWLEDGEMENTS

Soccer-mad Bareng Batho-Kortjaas appointed himself my time-keeper and writing coach, always demanding progress reports and insisting on going through what I had written.

A special 'thank you' to friends of mine who took the time to read earlier drafts of some of the chapters and make suggestions on how to improve them. They were also there to give me words of encouragement when the going seemed to be getting tough. Without you I would not have made it.

My family – especially my daughters Nothando and Keorapetse – has been incredibly understanding throughout the process, forgiving me for skipping family gatherings and cancelling trips at short notice. *Bo Nomndayi, Singila!*

I was fortunate to have as my editor Frances Perryer, whose suggestions helped me improve the work while not interfering with my voice.

All the mistakes are, however, mine.

S'thembiso Msomi
Johannesburg
May 2016

Notes

INTRODUCTION

1. Mmusi Maimane, DA mayoral candidate for Johannesburg, 21 March 2011, https://www.youtube.com/watch?v=EJQuzEbie6k.
2. Ibid.
3. Zille speaking at a press conference to unveil Maimane as the new party spokesman, December 2012.
4. Greg Nicolson, 'Mmusi Maimane wins DA leadership race', *Daily Maverick*, 10 May 2015.
5. Mmusi Maimane's first address as DA federal leader, 10 May 2015.
6. *City Press*, 18 June 2014.
7. Ibid.
8. Gareth van Onselen, 'Julius Malema: the real leader of the opposition', *Business Day*, 25 August 2014.
9. Ibid.
10. Ibid.
11. Interview with Makashule Gana, 23 September 2015.
12. Mmusi Maimane addressing the British Chamber of Business in Southern Africa meeting, Inanda Club, 16 July 2015.
13. Ibid.

CHAPTER 1

1. Interview with Ian Ollis, DA MP, 30 September 2015.
2. http://www.news24.com/myviews24/yourstory.
3. Marianne Merten and Donwald Pressly, 'DA moves to attract more black voters', IOL, 2 October 2011.
4. Interview with Ollis, 30 September 2015
5. Ibid.
6. Almost everyone who has known Maimane outside of politics and his Dobsonville neighbourhood says they were first introduced to him as Aloysias.
7. Riaan Wolmarans, Matthew Burbidge, 'Zuma is the new ANC president', Sapa-AFP, http://mg.co.za/article/2007-12-18-zuma-is-new-anc-president .
8. Since Zuma's victory at Polokwane, the ANC has seen some of its members break away to form the Congress of the People (in 2008) and the Economic Freedom Fighters (in 2013). Its trade union federation alliance partner, Cosatu, has also suffered a split with its majority union, the National Union of Metalworkers of South Africa (Numsa) being expelled for refusing to encourage its members to vote for the ANC.
9. 'Focus on the challenges facing our people', Statement by ANC president Jacob Zuma on behalf of the National Executive Committee, www.anc.org.za, 22 September 2008.
10. The ANC NEC meeting that removed Mbeki from office took place in September 2008, some eight months before the general elections that would have marked the official end to his second and final term as the country's president.
11. Interview with Fikile-Ntsikelelo Moya, 23 August 2015.
12. Interview with Thabo Shole-Mashao, 12 November 2015.
13. 'A million reasons for the DA's newfound love for Thabo Mbeki', http://www.dailymaverick.co.za/article/2014-03-31-a-million-reasons-for-the-das-newfound-love-for-thabo-mbeki/#.V1FMJhHyXrc,
14. Interview with Shole-Mashao, 12 November 2015.
15. S'thembiso Hlongwane, *Destiny Man*, August 2015.
16. 'Towards a new political identity', Maimane's speech on race and identity delivered at the Apartheid Museum, 20 February 2014.
17. Sophie Tema, 'Where no one dares to walk', *City Press*, 27 September 1992.

NOTES

18 Interview with local resident Kgotla Molefe, 8 November 2015.
19 Ibid.
20 Interview with Fikile-Ntsikelelo Moya, 23 August 2015.
21 Fikile-Ntsikelelo Moya and Thabo Shole-Mashao, in separate interviews, name the late Sister Christine as a great influence in their and Maimane's lives.
22 Ibid.
23 Maimane in an interview with *Noseweek*, 1 May 2015.
24 Interview with Shole-Mashao, 11 November 2015.
25 See for instance 'Writing in the time of racism' by Subry Govender, www.thejournalist.org.za.
26 'Bringing hope and dignity to South African girls', a profile on Shole-Mashao by Rams Mabote, *Dubbo Weekender*, 1 December 2012.
27 Ibid.
28 Interview with Ollis, 30 September 2015.
29 Interview with Patricia de Lille, 19 December 2015.
30 Statement by DA leader Helen Zille on the realignment of politics, 11 December 2011.
31 Maimane's address at the Heritage Day Celebrations in Pretoria, 24 September 2014.
32 'More than just a token', Maimane's interview with *BBQ* magazine, Issue 65, July 2015.
33 Interview with Shole-Mashao, 12 November 2015.
34 'I have a dream', Sue Segar, *Noseweek*, 1 May 2015.
35 Video of Maimane's sermon at Liberty Church, April 2015.
36 Ibid.
37 Interview with Ollis, 30 September 2015.
38 In the same year that Maimane became DA leader, the ANC Youth League elected Collen Maine its president just two weeks before his thirty-fifth birthday.
39 Donwald Pressly, *Owning the future: Lindiwe Mazibuko and the changing face of the DA*, Kwela Books, 2014.
40 Raenette Taljaard, *Up in Arms: Pursuing accountability for the Arms Deal in Parliament*, Jacana, 2012.
41 Interview with Ollis, 30 September 2015.

42 Ibid.
43 Zille's speech in Johannesburg as she announced the party's mayoral candidate for the city, 15 May 2015.
44 Gareth van Onselen, http://www.bdlive.co.za/opinion/columnists/2014/04/22/mmusi-maimane-the-hollow-man.
45 Ibid.
46 Interview with Ollis, 30 September 2015.
47 Ibid.

CHAPTER 2

1 Interview with Thabo Shole-Mashao, 2 November 2015.
2 Ibid.
3 Interview with Kgotla Molefe, who grew up with Maimane as a neighbour.
4 Mkokeli Sam, 'The Soweto "nice guy" who would be DA king', *Sunday Times*, 4 May 2015.
5 Maimane's official CV.
6 Ibid.
7 Interview with Kgotla Molefe.
8 Maimane in his maiden speech as DA leader on 10 May 2015, in Port Elizabeth.
9 Ibid.
10 Ibid.
11 For instance, he did the same during his visit to Butterworth on 14 November 2015.
12 Dr HF Verwoerd, Minister for Native Affairs, addressing the Senate, 7 July 1954.
13 Companions of Saint Angela Merici, Constitutions, 1977.
14 http://www.sahistory.org.za/topic/june-16-soweto-youth-uprising-timeline-1976-1986.
15 Maimane's speech on race and identity, delivered at the Apartheid Museum, 19 February 2014.
16 Ibid.

NOTES

17 Interviews with Shole-Mashao and Kgotla Molefe.
18 'I have a dream', Sue Segar, *Noseweek*, May 2015.
19 *GQ* magazine, October 2015.
20 Interview with Kgotla Molefe.
21 'I have a dream', Sue Segar, *Noseweek*, May 2015.
22 Ibid.
23 *GQ* magazine, October 2015.
24 *Sawubona* (Zulu greeting: 'I see you are not my enemy'), Aloysias Maimane, 21 March 2007.
25 Kwanele Sosibo, 'Parliament: Culture no longer the trump card', *Mail & Guardian*, 5 December 2014.
26 Donwald Pressly, *Owning the future: Lindiwe Mazibuko and the changing face of the DA*, p 25.
27 Interview with Kgotla Molefe.
28 'I have a dream', Sue Segar, *Noseweek*, May 2015.
29 Interview with Thabo Shole-Mashao, 2 November 2015.
30 Ibid.
31 'Court battles like soccer – Maimane', News24, 8 October 2015.
32 Ibid.
33 *Sowetan*, 5 October 2012.
34 Interviews with Shole-Mashao, Moya and Kgotla Molefe.
35 'Allen Glen High School Celebrates 21 Years', 31 October 2014, www.roodepoortnorthsider.co.za.
36 'I have a dream', Sue Segar, *Noseweek*, May 2015.
37 Ibid.
38 WEB Du Bois, *The Souls of Black Folk*, 'Of Our Spiritual Strivings'. Chicago: AC McClurg & Co, 1903, p 3.
39 Semi-private multi-racial 'Model C' schools were abolished after the end of apartheid, but the term is still used to describe government schools reserved for the privileged and tending to produce better academic results.
40 Interview with Thabo Shole-Mashao, 2 November 2015.
41 S'thembiso Hlongwane, 'Mission Possible', *Destiny Magazine*, Issue 46.
42 *Monocle Magazine*, Volume 9, October 2015, p 74.

CHAPTER 3

1 'A broken man, presiding over a broken society', speech by Mmusi Maimane, 17 February 2015, https://www.da.org.za/2015/02/broken-man-presiding-broken-society/.
2 In his reply, Zuma ignored the DA leader and instead devoted a significant part of his speech to dispelling Freedom Front Plus claims that Afrikaners were under attack from the ANC-led government, http://www.gov.za/speeches/president-jacob-zuma-response-debate-state-nation-address-19-feb-2015-0000.
3 Zuma's reply to questions during a 28 May 2015 parliamentary sitting. https://www.youtube.com/watch?v=XeWXOn-rW60.
4 For instance during a Johannesburg City Council debate a month before the 2014 general election, Maimane said the millions spent on Zuma's home could have been used for housing and basic services in Soweto, http://www.news24.com/Elections/News/Maimane-Nkandla-funds-could-have-paid-for-services-20140416, 16 April 2014.
5 'Secure In Comfort', Report on an investigation into allegations of impropriety and unethical conduct relating to the installation and implementation of security measures by the Department of Public Works at and in respect of the private residence of President Jacob Zuma at Nkandla in the KwaZulu-Natal province. Report No 25 of 2013/14.
6 Sam Mkokeli, 'Maimane knows what he's in it for', *Sunday Times*, 19 April 2015.
7 'Who is the best speaker in parliament?', www.thevoiceclinic.co.za, 29 August 2014.
8 Interview with Jan-Jan Joubert, September 2015.
9 Gareth van Onselen, 'The DA's Manchurian candidate', *Business Day*, 13 April 2015.
10 Gareth van Onselen, 'Mmusi Maimane: the Hollow Man', *Business Day*, 22 April 2015.
11 Interview with Patricia de Lille, December 2015.
12 'More Highlights from Pretoria', 29 August 2006, http://familylifeblogs.blogspot.co.za/.
13 Interview with David Seletisha, former producer at Crux.
14 www.heartlines.org.za.
15 Ibid.

NOTES

16 https://www.youtube.com/watch?v=khoEfn-5Vzo.
17 http://ewn.co.za/2014/04/16/DA-vs-SABC-censored-adverts-SABC-argues-Nkandla-adverts-be-banned.
18 Icasa rules against DA advert, http://news.iafrica.com/sa/920459.html.
19 SU impacted my life, Aloysias Maimane, http://www.su.org.za/downloads/magazine/SU360-July07.pdf
20 http://www.speakersinc.co.za/component/content/article/98-m/409-musi-maimane.html.
21 www.tomorrowtodayglobal.com/2007/07/25/the-soul-of-your-african-celebration.
22 Maimane's status at the company was confirmed by TomorrowToday's operations director Jude Foulson in an e-mail to the author.
23 'The soul of your African: Celebration', Aloysias Maimane, 25 July 2007, www.tomorrowtodayglobal.com.
24 Ibid.
25 Mmusi Maimane addressing party supporters in Bethlehem, 4 October 2015.
26 Aloysias Maimane, 'The war for black talent', 28 September 2006.
27 Aloysias Maimane, 'Buppies – coming to terms with young black staff', 30 May 2007.
28 Ibid.
29 Maimane spoke about this idea of 'commuting' between the 'black and the white world' as a Model C schoolchild living in a township in his interview with *Noseweek*, 1 May 2015.
30 Aloysias Maimane, 'SU impacted my life', *Scripture Union Magazine*, Volume 360, July 2007.
31 Interview with Gana, 23 September 2015.

CHAPTER 4

1 Mmusi Maimane's first speech as DA leader, 10 May 2015.
2 'Rat attack puts Alex baby in hospital', Eyewitness News, 27 August 2014.
3 Rodent Control Strategy 2011–2015, Ekurhuleni Municipality.
4 Ibid.
5 Murray Williams, 'We blacks are no puppets', 21 May 2014.

6 Khaya Dlanga, 'Obamafication of Maimane won't earn DA the black vote', *Mail & Guardian*, 1 May 2014.
7 BBC HARDtalk interview, 30 June 2015.
8 DA media statement, 22 December 2015.
9 Interview with De Lille, Cape Town, December 2015.
10 Maimane in an interview on SAFM, 22 December 2015.
11 Mmusi Maimane, 'Dear Penny Sparrow and others', *Daily Maverick*, 10 January 2016.
12 Aubrey Matshiqi, 'More prayers to patron of hopeless causes needed', *Business Day*, 1 December 2015.
13 Sam Mkokeli, 'Maimane's failure to act on race tars the DA's image', *Business Day*, 11 January 2016.
14 Zuma's remarks during an interview with e NCA journalist Thulasizwe Simelane, January 2016.
15 Zuma speaking at the TNA Breakfast hosted by the SABC to mark the ANC's 104th anniversary in January 2016.
16 'Let's find each other', Mmusi Maimane's speech on race and identity at the Apartheid Museum, 19 January 2016.
17 Niq Mhlongo, *After Tears*, as quoted from Maimane's speech.
18 Interview with Ian Ollis, 30 September 2015.
19 The DA's anti-racism pledge as read out by Maimane, 19 January 2016.
20 'DA leader has a plan to change the party's complexion', *Sunday Times*, 24 January 2016.
21 Lindiwe Mazibuko, 'Maimane race plan must be incorporated in DA', *Business Day*, 21 January 2016.

CHAPTER 5

1 An interview with Maimane outside Bohlokong New Community Hall, 4 October 2015.
2 Dihlabeng local government spokeswoman Tsediso Maitse gave this explanation in an interview with Media 24, http://www.news24.com/southafrica/local/express-news/opposition-locked-out-20151006.
3 Ibid.

NOTES

4   Patricia Kopane, DA leader in the Free State, addressing party supporters at the Bohlokong New Community Hall.
5   Maimane addressing party supporters at the Bohlokong New Community Hall.
6   Mia Malan, 'It's the Free State Hospital that killed my husband, Frik', *Mail & Guardian*, 20 May 2015.
7   This was in reference to 2013 reports that the provincial government had signed a R105-million contract with businessman Tumi Ntsele to redesign its website. Free State director general Elzabe Rockman later disputed the amount, saying the province had only spent R40-million on the project.
8   Babalo Ndenze and Jan-Jan Joubert, 'Demotion for Kohler Barnard over PW post', *Sunday Times*, 4 October 2015.
9   Ibid.
10 Press conference in Bohlokong, Bethlehem, 4 October 2015.
11 Changes to DA shadow cabinet, DA statement, 3 October 2015.
12 @MolotoMothapo, 1 October 2015.
13 @helenzille, 1 October 2015.
14 @MmusiMaimane, 1 October 2015.
15 Maimane speaking after the Bohlokong rally, 4 October 2015.
16 Murray Williams, 'We are a South African family', *Cape Argus*, 14 August 2014.
17 Mapula Nkosi, 'Crazy little thing called love knows no colour', *Sowetan*, 3 October 2014.
18 Murray Williams, 'We are a South African family', *Cape Argus*, 14 August 2014.
19 'On Race and Identity', Mmusi Maimane's speech at the Apartheid Museum, 19 February 2014.
20 Ibid.
21 Murray Williams, 'We are a South African family', *Cape Argus*, 14 August 2014.
22 Sam Mkokeli, 'The Soweto nice guy who would be DA king: Mmusi Maimane', *Sunday Times*, 4 May 2015.
23 Ibid.
24 Maimane documentary, eNCA, Facebook, May 2015.
25 Ibid.

26 Facebook video of Natalie Maimane's interview with Netwerk24.
27 Stone Setumo, 'ANC abandoned reconciliation', *City Press*, 20 January 2016.
28 'Concerns around the comments that you made to a number of delegates at the federal congress in PE', letter by Athol Trollip to Bonginkosi Madikizela.
29 Jan-Jan Joubert, 'Maimane "not black enough" letter rocks the DA', *Sunday Times*, 22 November 2015.
30 Bianca Capazorio, 'I'm no Hillary Clinton, says Mrs Maimane', *Sunday Times*, 31 May 2015.

CHAPTER 6

1 www.elections.org.za.
2 http://www.elections.org.za/content/Elections/Results/2014-National-and-Provincial-Elections--Gauteng-results/
3 Interview with De Lille, December 2015.
4 Maimane's acceptance speech, 10 May 2015, DA federal congress, Port Elizabeth.
5 Speaking to Maimane at Gelvandale Stadium, Port Elizabeth, November 2015.
6 Interview with Trollip at Gelvandale Stadium, Port Elizabeth, November 2015
7 Trollip at the Gelvandale Stadium rally in Port Elizabeth, November 2015.
8 Interview with Ian Ollis, 30 September 2015.
9 'Arrogance cost ANC Mandela Bay ward', *The Herald*, 21 August 2015.
10 Ibid.
11 'Racism must fall for DA to succeed', Mcebisi Ndletyana, *Sunday Independent*, 15 November 2015.
12 Ibid.
13 Interview with Solly Msimanga, *Sunday Times* offices, October 2015.
14 Young Professionals Debate, 26 October 2015.
15 Ibid.
16 Ibid.

NOTES

CHAPTER 7

1. Interview with Makashule Gana, 23 September 2015.
2. This is according to Maimane in a conversation with the author in July 2015.
3. A phrase used by Athol Trollip during an interview with the author, Port Elizabeth, 15 November 2015.
4. 'Maimane's no Zille, says Malema', www.iol.co.za, 24 April 2015.
5. 'Maimane will turn DA into a church: Malema', Times LIVE, 24 April 2015.
6. 'Zille still in charge of DA – Malema', www.news24.com, 24 April 2016.
7. Babalo Ndenze, 'Maimane dismisses Juju as populist', *Cape Times*, 10 July 2014.
8. 'Malema and Maimane slug it out for black votes', *Sunday Times*, 8 November 2015.
9. 'DA will not enter into any coalition with EFF', Helen Zille statement, 23 April 2014.
10. Maimane outlined his conditions for a future coalition agreement with other opposition parties at a meeting with the British Chamber of Business in Southern Africa, at the Inanda Club, Sandton, in July 2015.
11. 'Malema and Maimane slug it out for black votes', *Sunday Times*, 8 November 2015.

CHAPTER 8

1. Zille's press statement announcing the collapse of her deal with Ramphele, 2 February 2014.
2. 'Fire and ice', *City Press*, 19 May 2013.
3. Interview with De Lille, December 2015.
4. Zille's press statement announcing the collapse of her deal with Ramphele, 2 February 2014.
5. Interview with De Lille, December 2015.
6. Interview with Makashule Gana, September 2015.
7. Maimane's BBC HARDTalk interview, 1 July 2015.
8. Debate between Maimane and James, 'Insig', kykNET, 5 May 2015.
9. Ibid.

10 Genevieve Quintal, 'Maimane, James in mudslinging battle', News24, 7 May 2015.
11 Ibid.
12 Ibid.
13 Maimane's Facebook post, 6 May 2015.
14 Siya Khumalo, 'What just happened, @MmusiMaimane?', https://sanitythinksoutloud.com/?s=mmusi+maimane, 6 May 2015.
15 Aloysias Maimane's sermon at Liberty Church, https://www.youtube.com/watch?v=dNONZik49wQ.
16 Tweet by @MmusiMaimane, 14 May 2015.
17 Interview with Ian Ollis, 30 September 2015.
18 Ibid.
19 Breakfast with the next leader of the DA? Eusebius McKaiser talks sex, drugs and non-racialism with Mmusi Maimane, 29 April 2015.
20 'The unAfrican liberal', *City Press*, 3 February 2013.
21 Songezo Zibi, *Raising the bar – hope & renewal in South Africa*, Picador Africa, 2014.
22 Lindiwe Mazibuko, 'Maimane race plan must be incorporated in DA', *Business Day*, 21 January 2016.
23 S Booysen, *Dominance and decline, the ANC in the time of Zuma*, Wits University Press, 2015.
24 Tweet by @MmusiMaimane, 9 January 2013.
25 Interview with De Lille, December 2015.
26 'The unAfrican liberal', *City Press*, 3 February 2013.
27 Interview with Ollis, 30 September 2015.
28 Breakfast with next leader of the DA? Eusebius McKaiser talks sex, drugs and non-racialism with Mmusi Maimane, 29 April 2015.
29 Eddie Maloka, 'Racial denialism in liberal drag', *Sunday Independent*, 1 December 2013.
30 'Some notes on liberalism', Z Pallo Jordan, *Focus 63*, Helen Suzman Foundation.
31 Ibid.
32 Quoted from Merle Lipton, 'Liberals, Marxists, and Nationalists, competing interpretations of South African history', *How Historians Shape History*, 2007, p 139.

NOTES

33 Michael Cardo, 'The liberal tradition in South Africa: Past and present', *Focus* 63, Helen Suzman Foundation.
34 Ibid.
35 Ibid.
36 Ibid.
37 Ibid.
38 Ibid.

CHAPTER 9

1 'Rand Stadium rises from the ashes', http://www.southafrica.info/2010/project2010column47.htm#.V1FS6hHyXrc.
2 Football in South Africa Timeline 1862–2012, South African History Online, www.sahistory.org.za/topic/football-south-africa-timeline-1862-2012.
3 Ibid.
4 Lindiwe Mazibuko's election diary, 30 March 2011.
5 Maimane's speech at the DA local government manifesto launch rally, 23 April 2016.
6 Ibid.
7 Ibid.
8 Ibid.
9 Maimane's address at a DA rally in Cape Town, 1 May 2016.
10 DA Policy on Economic Inclusion, December 2013.
11 'Our nation would be in a better state with the DA's 15 ministries', address by Maimane at the Cape Town Press Club, 10 February 2016.
12 The list is lifted from Maimane's speech: 'Our nation would be in a better state with the DA's 15 ministries', address to the Cape Town Press Club, 10 February 2016.
13 Mbeki was quoted by journalist Carol Paton in the article 'Mmusi Maimane: Can he change the DA?' *Financial Mail*, 16 April 2015.
14 Mmusi Maimane, 'SA needs change that creates jobs', *Bokamoso*, 8 January 2016.
15 Ibid.

16 Ibid.
17 According to former ANC Gauteng secretary (now premier) David Makhura in an interview with the *Sunday Times* in April 2014, 'ANC turns to Mbeki for help'.
18 Sibongakonke Shoba, 'ANC concedes it lost middle class in Gauteng', *Sunday Times*, 24 August 2014.
19 'Black professionals and the ANC in the 2014 election: Loosening ties?', *Elections 2014 – the campaigns, results and the future prospects*, edited by Collette Schulz-Herzenberg and Roger Southall, Jacana, 2014, pp 155–168.
20 Ibid.
21 Mmusi Maimane, 'The DA's version of BEE will deliver real Black Economic Empowerment', *Bokamoso*, 26 January 2016.
22 Ibid.
23 Ibid.
24 'Black professionals and the ANC in the 2014 election: Loosening ties?', *Elections 2014 – the campaigns, results and the future prospects*, edited by Collette Schulz-Herzenberg and Roger Southall, Jacana, pp 155–168.
25 'DA reports Speaker and ANC MPs who voted to protect Zuma to Ethics Committee', DA statement, 7 April 2016.

Bibliography

BACKGROUND READING

Cardo, Michael, *Opening men's eyes: Peter Brown and the Liberal struggle for South Africa*, Jonathan Ball Publishers, 2010.

—, 'The liberal tradition in South Africa: Past and present', *Focus 63*, Helen Suzman Foundation, November 2011.

Du Bois, WEB, *The Souls of Black Folks*, 'Of Our Spiritual Strivings', AC McClurg & Co, 1903, p 3.

Forde, Fiona, *Still an inconvenient youth: Julius Malema carries on*, Picador Africa, 2011.

Helen Suzman Foundation, 'On liberty, SA Liberalism', *Focus 65*, Helen Suzman Foundation, July 2012.

Maloka, Eddy, *Friends of the natives, the inconvenient past of South African Liberalism*, 3rd Millenium, 2014.

McKaiser, Eusebius, *Could I vote DA? – A voter's dilemma*, Bookstorm, 2014.

Lipton, Merle, 'Liberals, Marxists, and Nationalists, competing interpretations of South African history', *How Historians Shape History*, Palgrave Macmillan, 2007.

Pressly, Donwald, *Owning the Future: Lindiwe Mazibuko and the changing face of the DA*, Kwela Books, 2013.

Public Protector, 'Secure In Comfort', Report on an investigation into allegations of impropriety and unethical conduct relating to the installation and implementation of security measures by the Department of Public Works at and in respect of the private residence of President Jacob Zuma at Nkandla in the KwaZulu-Natal province. Report No 25 of 2013/14.

Taljaard, Raenette, *Up in arms: Pursuing accountability for the Arms Deal in Parliament*, Jacana, 2012.

BOOKS, MAGAZINE AND NEWSPAPER ARTICLES

Booysen, Susan, *Dominance and decline, the ANC in the time of Zuma*, Wits University Press, 2015.

Capazorio, Bianca, 'I'm no Hillary Clinton, says Mrs Maimane', *Sunday Times*, 31 May 2015.

Capazorio, Bianca and Sibongakonke Shoba, 'Malema and Maimane slug it out for black votes', *Sunday Times*, 8 November 2015.

Companions of Saint Angela Merici, Constitutions, 1977.

Democratic Alliance, Policy on Economic Inclusion, December 2013, https://www.da.org.za/why-the-da/policies/job-business/economic-inclusion-policy/.

—, Ad campaign, https://www.youtube.com/watch?v=khoEfn-5Vzo, 2014.

—, Ad campaign, http://ewn.co.za/2014/04/16/DA-vs-SABC-censored-adverts-SABC-argues-Nkandla-adverts-be-banned, 2014.

—, Statement: Changes to DA shadow cabinet, 3 October 2015, https://www.da.org.za/2015/10/changes-to-da-shadow-cabinet/.

—, Press conference in Bohlokong, Bethlehem, 4 October 2015, https://www.da.org.za/2015/10/vision-2029-use-your-vote-to-elect-a-government-that-cares/.

—, Anti-racism pledge as read out by Maimane, 19 January 2016, https://www.da.org.za/2016/01/lets-find-each-other-again/.

—, Statement: 'DA reports Speaker and ANC MPs who voted to protect Zuma to Ethics Committee', 7 April 2016, https://www.da.org.za/2016/04/da-reports-speaker-and-anc-mps-who-voted-to-protect-zuma-to-ethics-committee/.

Dlanga, Khaya, 'Obamafication of Maimane won't earn DA the black vote', *Mail & Guardian*, 1 May 2014.

BIBLIOGRAPHY

Electoral Commission of South Africa, http://www.elections.org.za/content/Elections/Results/2014-National-and-Provincial-Elections--Gauteng-results/.

Du Plessis, Carien, 'The unAfrican liberal', *City Press*, 3 February 2013.

Govender, Subry, 'Writing in a time of racism', Issue 37, www.thejournalist.org.za.

Grootes, Stephen, 'A million reasons for the DA's newfound love for Thabo Mbeki', http://www.dailymaverick.co.za/article/2014-03-31-a-million-reasons-for-the-das-newfound-love-for-thabo-mbeki/#.V1FMJhHyXrc.

Harrisberg, Monique, 'Who is the best speaker in parliament?', www.thevoiceclinic.co.za, 29 August 2014.

Hlongwane, S'thembiso, 'Mission possible', *Destiny Magazine*, Issue 46, August 2015.

Jordan, Z Pallo, 'Some notes on liberalism', *Focus 63*, Helen Suzman Foundation, November 2011.

Joubert, Jan-Jan, 'Maimane "not black enough" letter rocks the DA', *Sunday Times*, 22 November 2015.

Khumalo, Siya, 'What just happened, @MmusiMaimane?', https://sanitythinksoutloud.com/?s=mmusi+maimane, 6 May 2015.

Mabote, Rams, 'Bringing hope and dignity to South African girls', *Dubbo Weekender*, 1 December 2012.

Maimane, Mmusi Aloysias, Official CV, Democratic Alliance, 2015.

—, 'The war for black talent', www.tomorrowtoday.com, 28 September 2006.

—, 'Buppies – coming to terms with young black staff', www.tomorrowtodayglobal.com, 30 May 2007.

—, 'SU impacted my life', *Scripture Union Magazine*, Volume 360, July 2007, http://www.su.org.za/downloads/magazine/SU360-July07.pdf.

—, *Sawubona* (Zulu greeting: 'I see you are not my enemy'), www.tomorrowtodayglobal.com, 21 March 2007.

—, 'The soul of your African: Celebration', www.tomorrowtodayglobal.com, 25 July 2007.

—, DA mayoral candidate, Johannesburg, 21 March 2011, https://www.youtube.com/watch?v=EJQuzEbie6k.

—, 'Towards a new political identity', speech on race and identity at the Apartheid Museum, 20 February 2014, https://www.da.org.za/2014/02/towards-a-new-political-identity/.

—, Johannesburg City Council debate, http://www.news24.com/Elections/News/

Maimane-Nkandla-funds-could-have-paid-for-services-20140416, 16 April 2014.
—, Address, Heritage Day Celebrations, Pretoria, 24 September 2014, copies of the speech distributed to the media on the day.
—, 'A broken man, presiding over a broken society', 17 February 2015, https://www.da.org.za/2015/02/broken-man-presiding-broken-society/.
—, Debate between Maimane and Wilmot James, 'Insig', kykNET, 5 May 2015.
—, Address, first speech as DA federal leader, 10 May 2015, http://www.news24.com/SouthAfrica/News/Mmusi-Maimanes-first-speech-as-DA-leader-20150510.
—, Documentary, eNCA, Facebook, May 2015, http://www.speakersinc.co.za/component/content/article/98-m/409-musi-maimane.html.
—, BBC HARDtalk interview, 30 June 2015, https://www.youtube.com/watch?v=3hdZ5rJScIo.
—, 'More than just a token', *BBQ* magazine, Issue 65, July 2015.
—, Address to British Chamber of Business in Southern Africa meeting, Inanda Club, 16 July 2015, https://www.da.org.za/2015/07/to-protect-our-democracy-we-must-protect-our-institutions/.
—, 'The man in the middle, Mmusi Maimane', Craig Tyson, GQ magazine, October 2015.
—, 'Q&A: Mmusi Maimane, leader of the Democratic Alliance', Alexander Matthews, *Monocle Magazine*, Volume 9, October 2015, p 74.
—, 'Court battles like soccer – Maimane', News24, 8 October 2015.
—, Interview, SAFM, 22 December 2015, http://www.sabc.co.za/news/a/4c5397004b08b43281a3eb445cadceaa/Kohler-Barnard-recognises-the-seriousness-of-her-actions:-Maimane-20152212.
—, Sermon, Liberty Church, https://www.youtube.com/watch?v=dNONZik49wQ.
—, 'SA needs change that creates jobs', *Bokamoso*, 8 January 2016.
—, 'Dear Penny Sparrow and others', *Daily Maverick*, 10 January 2016.
—, 'Let's find each other', speech on race and identity at the Apartheid Museum, 19 January 2016, http://www.polity.org.za/article/da-mmusi-maimane-address-by-da-leader-during-his-speech-on-speech-on-race-and-identity-in-the-da-and-in-south-africa-apartheid-museum-johannesburg-19012016-2016-01-19.

BIBLIOGRAPHY

—, 'The DA's version of BEE will deliver real Black Economic Empowerment', *Bokamoso*, 26 January 2016.

—, 'Our nation would be in a better state with the DA's 15 ministries', address to the Cape Town Press Club, 10 February 2016, https://www.da.org.za/2016/02/bokamoso-special-edition-our-nation-would-be-in-a-better-state-with-the-das-15-ministries/.

—, Speech at the DA local government manifesto launch rally, 23 April 2016, https://www.da.org.za/campaign/2016-local-government-elections-manifesto/.

—, Address, DA May Day rally, Cape Town, 1 May 2016, www.da.org.za.

Makhura, David, 'ANC turns to Mbeki for help', interview, *Sunday Times*, April 2014.

Malema, Julius, 'Maimane will turn DA into a church: Malema', Times LIVE, 24 April 2015.

—, 'Maimane's no Zille, says Malema', www.iol.co.za, 24 April 2015.

—, 'Zille still in charge of DA – Malema', www.news24.com, 24 April 2015.

Maloka, Eddie, 'Racial denialism in liberal drag', *Sunday Independent*, 1 December 2013.

Matshiqi, Aubrey, 'More prayers to patron of hopeless causes needed', *Business Day*, 1 December 2015.

Mazibuko, Lindiwe Election diary, 30 March 2011. www.da.org.za.

—, 'Maimane race plan must be incorporated in DA', *Business Day*, 21 January 2016.

Mbeki, Moeletsi, quoted by Carol Paton, 'Mmusi Maimane: Can he change the DA?' *Financial Mail*, 16 April 2015.

McKaiser, Eusebius, Breakfast with the next leader of the DA?, Eusebius McKaiser talks sex, drugs and non-racialism with Mmusi Maimane, 29 April 2015, http://www.iol.co.za/news/breakfast-with-next-leader-of-the-da-1851825.

Merten, Marianne and Donwald Pressly, 'DA moves to attract more black voters', IOL, 2 October 2011.

Mhlongo, Niq, *After Tears*, Ohio University Press, 2011.

Mkokeli, Sam, 'Maimane knows what he's in it for', *Sunday Times*, 19 April 2015.

—, 'The Soweto "nice guy" who would be DA king', *Sunday Times*, 4 May 2015.

—, 'Maimane's failure to act on race tars the DA's image', *Business Day*, 11 January 2016.

Ndenze, Babalo, 'Maimane dismisses Juju as populist', *Cape Times*, 10 July 2014.

Ndenze, Babalo and Jan-Jan Joubert, 'Demotion for Kohler Barnard over PW post', *Sunday Times*, 4 October 2015.

Ndletyana, Mcebisi, 'Racism must fall for DA to succeed', *Sunday Independent*, 15 November 2015.

Ngoma, Amuzweni, 'Black professionals and the ANC in the 2014 election: Loosening ties?', in *Elections 2014 – the campaigns, results and the future prospects*, edited by Collette Schulz-Herzenberg and Roger Southall, Jacana, 2014, pp 155–168.

Nicholson, Greg, 'Mmusi Maimane wins DA leadership race', *Daily Maverick*, 10 May 2015.

Nkosi, Mapula, 'Crazy little thing called love knows no colour', *Sowetan*, 3 October 2014.

Pressly, Donwald, *Owning the future: Lindiwe Mazibuko and the changing face of the DA*, Kwela Books, 2014.

Quintal, Genevieve, 'Maimane, James in mudslinging battle', News24, 7 May 2015. roodepoortnorthsider, 'Allen Glen High School Celebrates 21 years, 31 October 2014, www.roodepoortnorthsider.co.za.

Segar, Sue, 'I have a dream', *Noseweek*, 1 May 2015.

Setumo, Stone, 'ANC abandoned reconciliation', *City Press*, 20 January 2016.

Shoba, Sibongakonke, 'ANC concedes it lost middle class in Gauteng', *Sunday Times*, 24 August 2014.

Sosibo, Kwanele, 'Parliament: Culture no longer the trump card', *Mail & Guardian*, 5 December 2014.

South African History Online, http://www.sahistory.org.za/topic/june-16-soweto-youth-uprising-timeline-1976-1986.

Tabane, Rapule, 'Maimane charms Zuma while Malema turns up the heat', *City Press*, 18 June 2014.

Tema, Sophie, 'Where no one dares to walk', *City Press*, 27 September 1992.

Trollip, Athol, 'Concerns around the comments that you made to a number of delegates at the federal congress in PE', Letter to Bonginkosi Madikizela, undated.

van Onselen, Gareth, 'Julius Malema: the real leader of the opposition', *Business Day*, 25 August 2014.

—, 'The DA's Manchurian candidate', *Business Day*, 13 April 2015.

BIBLIOGRAPHY

—, 'Mmusi Maimane: the Hollow Man', *Business Day*, 22 April 2015.

Verwoerd, HF, Address to Senate, 7 July 1954.

Williams, Murray, 'We blacks are no puppets', 21 May 2014, http://www.iol.co.za/news/politics/we-da-blacks-are-no-puppets-1691343.

—, 'We are a South African family', *Cape Argus*, 14 August 2014.

Wolmarans, Riaan and Matthew Burbidge, 'Zuma is the new ANC president', Sapa-AFP, http://mg.co.za/article/2007-12-18-zuma-is-new-anc-president.

Young Professionals Debate, 26 October 2015, https://www.facebook.com/pages/DA-Young-Professionals-Network/282977685084579.

Zibi, Songezo, *Raising the bar – hope & renewal in South Africa*, Picador Africa, 2014.

Zille, Helen, Statement on the realignment of politics, 11 December 2011, http://www.polity.org.za/article/da-statement-by-helen-zille-democratic-alliance-leader-on-the-realignment-of-politics-11122011-2011-12-11.

—, Press conference unveiling Maimane as new DA spokesman, 13 December 2011, www.da.org.za.

—, Statement announcing collapse of deal with Ramphele, 2 February 2014, www.da.org.za.

—, Statement: 'DA will not enter into any coalition with EFF', 23 April 2014, https://www.da.org.za/newsroom/.

—, Announcement, DA mayoral candidate for Johannesburg, 15 May 2011, https://www.da.org.za/archive/2011-elections-da-announces-mayoral-candidates-for-city-of-johannesburg-and-tshwane-metro/.

Zuma, Jacob, 'Focus on the challenges facing our people', Statement on behalf of the National Executive Committee, www.anc.org.za, 22 September 2008.

—, Response to debate on State of Nation Address, http://www.gov.za/speeches/president-jacob-zuma-response-debate-state-nation-address-19-feb-2015-0000.

—, Reply to questions, 28 May 2015 parliamentary sitting. https://www.youtube.com/watch?v=XeWXOn-rW6o.

—, TNA Breakfast hosted by the SABC to mark ANC's 104th anniversary, January 2016.

—, Remarks during an interview with eNCA journalist Thulasizwe Simelane, January 2016.

INTERVIEWS

Athol Trollip, Port Elizabeth, 15 November 2015.
David Seletisha, telephonic interview, 16 October 2015.
Fikile-Ntsikelelo Moya, telephonic interview, 23 August 2015.
Ian Ollis, Rosebank, Johannesburg, 30 September 2015.
Jan-Jan Joubert, telephonic interview, 22 September 2015.
Kgotla Molefe, Dobsonville, Soweto, 8 November 2015.
Makashule Gana, Auckland Park, Johannesburg, 23 September 2015.
Patricia de Lille, Cape Town, 19 December 2015.
Solly Msimanga, *Sunday Times* offices, October 2015.
Thabo Shole-Mashao, telephonic interviews, 2 and 12 November 2015.

Index

affirmative action 28, 118–119
African National Congress (ANC)
   black middle class 162
   local government elections 39, 108
   Maimane's attempt to join 31, 34–35
   opposition parties and 92, 101–102, 104–105, 116
   president of 2–5, 22–24, 122–123
   support for 73, 91, 104, 107–113, 120, 122–124, 152
   Treason Trial 30
   Youth League 3–4, 123
After Tears 84
Agang SA 134–137
Alexandra township 73, 154
Al Jazeera 156
Allen Glen High School 50, 52–53
ANC *see* African National Congress
Apartheid Museum, Johannesburg 82–83
Atkinson, Patrick 35

Badawi, Zeinab 76
Bantu Education 43–45, 72, 155
Baron, Chris 138
BBC 76–77, 137
Beckett, Denis 118

BEE *see* Black Economic Empowerment
Bethlehem 90–93
Beyoncé 11
Black Consciousness Movement 53, 130, 135, 140
Black Economic Empowerment (BEE) 11, 28, 119, 158, 163–165
Black Like Me 118
#BlackLivesMatter campaign 155
Bobani, Mongameli 114
Bohlokong township 90–94
Bokamoso (blog) 163–164
Booysen, Johan 78
Booysen, Susan 145
Botha, PW 77, 78, 90, 98
broad-based black economic empowerment *see* Black Economic Empowerment
Brown, Peter 147, 148
Business Day 82, 88

cabinet portfolios 158–160
cadre deployment 17
Capazorio, Bianca 103
Cape Town 5, 110–111, 120, 157
Cape Town Press Club 127, 158–159

Cardo, Michael 147–148
Child in Crisis Foundation 69
City Press 13, 25, 135
Coetzee, Ryan 115
'colour-blind' vs non-racialism 9
  see also non-racialism
Companions of Saint Angela Merici 44
Congress of Democrats 30
Congress of South African Students (Cosas) 3, 116
Congress of the People (Cope) 5, 13, 24, 29, 31–32, 91, 110–111, 113, 162
Cosas *see* Congress of South African Students
Cosatu 2, 31, 113, 122, 162
Crux (TV programme) 63–64

DA *see* Democratic Alliance
Da Gama, Vasco 36
Daily Maverick 8
Dalindyebo, Buyelekhaya 94–96
De Beer, Zach 19
De Lille, Patricia 7, 28–29, 63, 81, 109, 120, 131, 136–137, 145
Democratic Alliance (DA)
  Agang SA and 134–137
  black middle class 162–165
  coalitions 17, 110–111, 112, 113, 117, 120–121, 127–128
  court cases 16, 50, 131–132
  diversity in 20, 87–89, 154–155
  EFF and 101–102, 117, 121, 124–130, 156, 165–166
  election targets 16–17, 37, 54–55, 106–117, 120–121, 129, 131, 151–155
  history of 144–148
  impeachment of Zuma 108, 132, 165
  leadership development in 34–35
  local government elections 5–7, 39, 157–158
  mayoral candidates 115–120
  Nkandla scandal 50, 131–133
  perceptions of voters 8, 30, 69–70, 73–75, 117
  policy issues 161–165
  poor black voters 160–162
  racial incidents 77–89, 94–98
  sexual misconduct, alleged 103–104, 137
  television ad campaigns 64–65
  Vision 2029 90, 94, 97, 154, 160
Democratic Party (DP) 9, 106–107, 144, 148
Deng Xiaoping 112
Destiny Man 24
Dihlabeng Regional Hospital 93–94
Dlamini-Zuma, Nkosazana 122, 123, 133
Dlanga, Khaya 12, 75–76
Dobsonville township 24–26, 41, 45–46, 50, 71–74, 100
DP *see* Democratic Party
'dual worlds' existence 53, 68–69
Duarte, Jessie 123
Du Bois, WEB 53

Economic Freedom Fighters (EFF)
  DA and 101–102, 117, 121, 124–130, 156, 165–166
  growth of 13–16, 35, 91, 104, 113, 115, 125–126, 128–130, 160, 162, 165–166
  Nkandla scandal 60, 132
  'respect for elders' 47–48
  State of the Nation Address 2015 56–57
education 43–45, 72, 155
EFF *see* Economic Freedom Fighters
Ekurhuleni 73–74, 109
eNCA 6, 83
e-tolls 104, 162
Evangelical Student Christian Movement 52

Facebook 140–141
  see also Kohler Barnard Facebook scandal

INDEX

Federation of International Football Associations (Fifa) 150
#FeesMustFall movement 54, 55
Fifa *see* Federation of International Football Associations
finance minister position 81
football *see* soccer
Freedom Charter 29–30, 151–152
Freedom Front Plus 91
Friedrich Naumann Foundation 115

Galanakis, Alec 53
Galanakis, Linda 52
Gana, Makashule 15–16, 70, 124, 137, 153, 160
Gauteng, elections in 5, 7, 37, 104, 109, 115–117, 120, 152
gay rights 140–142
Gigaba, Malusi 123
Gogotya, John 6
GQ South Africa 24
Grootes, Stephen 23–24
Gupta family 107–108

Hadebe, Thomas 97
HARDtalk 76–77, 137
Harrisberg, Monique 61
Heartlines 64
Hill-Lewis, Geordhin 140
Hope SA 35
hospitals *see* Dihlabeng Regional Hospital
housing 20–22

ID *see* Independent Democrats
Independent Communications Authority of SA 65
Independent Democrats (ID) 28–29, 136, 145

Jackson, Jesse 1
Jahed, Mohammed 32

James, Wilmot 7, 8, 134, 137–140
Jobs Campaign 161
Johannesburg 5, 7
Jonas, Mcebisi 108
Jordaan, Danny 111
Jordan, Pallo 122, 146–147
Joubert, Jan-Jan 62, 80, 168

Kaizer Chiefs 49–50, 151
Khomo, Thapelo 45–46
Khumalo, Siya 141
Khumalo, Theophilus 'Doctor' 49
Kirk, Paul 77–78
Kodwa, Zizi 113
Kohler Barnard Facebook scandal 77–81, 94, 95–97
Koornhof, Piet 150–151
Kopane, Patricia 92
kykNET debate 138–139, 142

labour legislation 119, 161–162
Lekota, Mosiuoa 29, 31–32, 111
Leon, Tony 86, 106, 144
Leratong Hospital 42
liberalism 138–149
Liberal Party 147
Liberals, Marxists, and Nationalists 146
Liberty Church 21, 32–34, 141, 142–143
Lipton, Merle 146
Luthuli, Albert 30, 149

Mackay, Gordon 35
Macufe (Mangaung African Cultural Festival) 67
Madikizela, Bonginkosi 103
Madisha, Willie 2
Madonsela, Thuli 50, 60, 107
Magashule, Ace 93–94
Maggs, Jeremy 6
Mahlangu, Solomon 116
Mail & Guardian 93

Maimane, Cecelia (sister) 45, 48, 52
Maimane, Ethel (mother) 42, 45, 52, 54
Maimane, Kabelo (brother) 45
Maimane, Kgalaletso (daughter) 97–98, 101
Maimane, Kgosi (son) 101
Maimane, Mmusi
   ANC, possible membership of 31, 34–35, 104–105
   career before politics 47, 63–69
   DA leadership positions 5–10, 19–24, 28–39, 137–143
   'dual worlds' existence 53, 68–69
   election targets 16–17, 55, 72–75, 90–94, 110, 117, 120, 129, 137, 152–158
   family of 42–43, 45–46, 52, 97–101
   impeachment of Zuma 108, 132, 165
   kind nature of 41–42, 48–49
   language proficiency 9, 25, 42
   Malema and 13–16, 59–61, 124–129
   marriage of 10, 42, 84, 98–105
   Mazibuko and 59–60
   names and nicknames of 21, 42, 48, 53, 61
   Nkandla scandal 60, 132–133
   on non-racialism 8–9, 29, 99, 102
   policy issues 32, 62, 69, 72, 118–119, 134, 138–149, 158–166
   presidential ambitions 123, 129, 131, 133
   public speaking skills 61–62
   'puppet' accusations 6, 11, 62–63, 75–77, 82, 87, 89, 106–107
   racial incidents 77–89, 94–98
   religious beliefs 32–34, 48–49, 51–53, 142–143
   'respect for elders' 46–48
   sexual misconduct, alleged 103–104, 137
   on social media 10–12, 75–76, 97, 140–141, 145
   sports 49–52
   State of the Nation Address 2015 56–59, 61–62
   university education 32, 33, 54
   youth of 24–28, 40–54
Maimane, Natalie (wife) 33, 35, 64, 97–105
Maimane, Simon (father) 42, 45–46, 52, 54
Maimane, Tumelo (sister) 45
Malakoane, Benny 93–94
Malema, Julius 3–4, 13–16, 56–59, 102, 124–130, 156, 165–166
Mali, Knight 114
Maloka, Eddie 146
Mandela, Nelson 8, 30, 84, 106, 156
Mangaung African Cultural Festival (Macufe) 67
Mantashe, Gwede 123
Mashaba, Herman 118–120
Matshiqi, Aubrey 82
Mazibuko, Lindiwe 7, 34, 38, 47–48, 59–60, 88, 102, 137, 144, 151–152, 163
Mbalula, Fikile 3, 76, 102, 123
Mbeki, Moeletsi 160
Mbeki, Thabo 2, 22–24, 76–77, 95, 156
Mbete, Baleka 47, 57, 108, 123, 131
Mbhele, Zakhele 96
Mbuli, Mzwakhe 26
McGough, Roger 85
Mchunu, Sizwe 78
McKaiser, Eusebius 143, 146
Mhlongo, Niq 84
middle class, black 162–165
Midvaal 120, 158
mission schools 43–44
Mkhize, Zweli 123
Mkokeli, Sam 61, 82
Mncwango, Zwakele 77–79, 81
'Model C' black voters 55
Modise, Thandi 57
Mofokeng, Saki 4
Mogoeng, Mogoeng 142
Mokaba, Peter 3
Mokonyane, Nomvula 26

INDEX

Molefe, Kgotla 25, 46, 48–49, 51, 52, 71–74, 100
Morake, Lilian 46
Morake, Matlhomola 46
Mothapo, Moloto 97
Motlanthe, Kgalema 77, 123
Motsoeneng, Hlaudi 50
Moya, Fikile-Ntsikelelo 22, 25–26, 51
Msimanga, Solly 115–117, 160
Msomi, Mandlenkosi Absolom 1–2

National Party (NP) 6, 106, 144
National Prosecutions Authority (NPA) 107
Nelson Mandela Bay Metropolitan Municipality 42–43, 109–115
Nene, Nhlanhla 81
Netwerk24 98, 99
New Africa Foundation 69
New Nation 26–27
New National Party (NNP) 86, 144
New Unity Movement 130
Ngoma, Amuzweni 163, 165
NGOs *see* non-governmental organisations
Nicholson, Chris 22
Nicolson, Greg 8
Nkandla scandal 15, 50, 56, 60, 64–65, 107, 124, 131–133, 162
Nkosi, Mapula 98
NNP *see* New National Party
non-governmental organisations (NGOs) 35, 69
non-racialism 8–9, 29, 99, 102
    see also race
Noseweek 26, 32
NP *see* National Party
NPA *see* National Prosecuting Authority
Nzimande, Blade 102

Obama, Barack 1–3, 61–62
Obotseng, Christine 26–28, 40–41

Ollis, Ian
    on liberalism 143, 145–146
    on Maimane's rise in DA 36–38, 86–88, 112, 131
    meets and recruits Maimane 19, 21–22, 28, 31, 34–35, 63
    Young Professionals Debate 118

PAC *see* Pan Africanist Congress
Pace Commercial Secondary School 51–53
Pan Africanist Congress (PAC) 73, 130
Pelser, Waldimar 138–139, 142
PFP *see* Progressive Federal Party
poor black voters 69–70, 120, 155, 160–162
Pringle, Thomas 146
Progressive Federal Party (PFP) 143, 147–148
Progressive Party 147–148
public debate on kykNET 138–139, 142
'puppet' accusations 6, 11, 62–63, 75–77, 82, 87, 89, 106–107

race
    non-racialism 9, 29, 99, 102
    racial inequality 84–85, 155–156
    racial mobilisation 10, 17, 106–107
    racism 77–89, 94–98, 114
Raising the bar 144
Ramaphosa, Cyril 122, 123, 133
Ramphele, Mamphela 134–137
Rand Stadium 150–154
rats 73–74
Roberts, Chris 114
rodent crisis 73–74
Roux, Barry 79
Rubusana, Thami 3

SABC 50, 63–65
SACP *see* South African Communist Party
sanitary towels, access to 27–28
Scripture Union (SU) 65–66, 68–69

Sebastian, Tim 77
Seletisha, David 63–64
Seremane, Joe 20
Sexwale, Tokyo 101
sex work 143
Shilowa, Mbhazima 32, 111
Shivambu, Floyd 47
Shoba, Sibongakonke 105, 168
Shole-Mashao, Thabo 23, 24, 26–28, 31, 40–41, 48–49, 51–53
Sisulu, Walter 30
Sisulu, Zwelakhe 26
Siyakholwa Development Foundation 69
Slabbert, Frederik van Zyl 19
Slabbert, Stanford 114
small businesses 157–158, 161, 164–165
soccer 49–50, 52, 150–151
social grants 10–11
social media
    Facebook 140–141
    Kohler Barnard Facebook scandal 77–81, 94, 95–97
    Maimane on 10–12, 75–76, 97, 140–141, 145
    Twitter 10–12, 76, 97, 145
Sokudela, Lutho 8
Solomon Mahlangu Square, Mamelodi Township 116
South African Communist Party (SACP) 30, 122
South African Indian Congress 30
Sowetan 52
Soweto uprising 44–45
Sparks, Allister 11
Sparrow, Penny 77, 81–83
Speakersinc.co.za 66, 68
sports 49–51, 52, 150–151
'Stand Up, Speak Out' initiative 85, 88–89
St Angela's Primary School 26, 40–41, 43–45
Star, The 143

State of the Nation Address 2015 56–59, 61–62
Steenhuisen, John 57
Stimela 45–46
SU *see* Scripture Union
Sunday Times 41, 88, 94, 103, 105, 138
Suzman, Helen 19, 144, 146

Tabane, Rapule 13–14
Taljaard, Raenette 34–35
Tambo, Oliver 30
tennis 50
Thusa a Girl Child (TaGC) movement 28
TomorrowToday Global 47, 66–68
Topham, Brandon 37
township violence 24–26
trade unions 162
transport system 158
Treason Trial 29–31, 154
Trollip, Athol 7, 20, 94, 103, 111–114
Tshabalala-Msimang, Manto 77
Tshwane 37, 109, 115–117, 120, 152
Tshwete, Mayihlome 12
Twitter 10–12, 76, 97, 145

UDM *see* United Democratic Movement
unemployment 69, 72, 157–158, 160–161
Unisa (University of South Africa) 54
United Democratic Movement (UDM) 29, 73, 112–113
United Front 113
University of South Africa (Unisa) 54

Van Damme, Phumzile 96
Van Onselen, Gareth 14–15, 32, 37, 62–63
Van Rooyen, David 'Des' 81
Van Schalkwyk, Marthinus 144
Vavi, Zwelinzima 2
Veeplaas township 112–113
Verwoerd, Hendrik 11, 43–44
Volmink, Heinrich 35

INDEX

Walter Sisulu Botanical Gardens 100
Walter Sisulu Square, Kliptown 151–152
Wayile, Zanoxolo 112
Western Cape *see* Cape Town
Wits University 32

youth development 69, 72

Zibi, Songezo 144
Zille, Helen
   growth of DA 20, 29, 86, 94, 106–107, 110, 115, 127, 134–137, 163
   Kohler Barnard Facebook scandal 97
   State of the Nation Address 2015 57
   steps down as party leader 33, 62, 109
   support for Maimane 5, 7–8, 36, 38
Zuma, Duduzane 108
Zuma, Jacob
   ANC presidency 2–5, 22–24
   finance minister position 81
   impact on support for ANC 104, 122, 133, 156, 165
   impeachment of 108, 132, 165
   Nkandla scandal 50, 107–108
   opposition parties and 14–15, 46, 83, 94
   State of the Nation Address 2015 58–59